"For many in the 1960s, Francis Schaeffer was the great door opener—opening the door to regaining the lordship of Christ over the whole of life and culture. For me personally, he stood head and shoulders above most others because of the way he took God so seriously, people so seriously, and truth so seriously. A flawed human being as we all are, he was a giant of the faith to whom we owe more than many people realize."

—**OS GUINNESS**, Author, Speaker, and Social Critic

"One of my most vivid memories of Schaeffer was waiting for him to arrive at our small London apartment where a group of students had met to hear him speak. Schaeffer was an hour late because he had been outside in the taxi talking to the driver about the Christian gospel! But this incident exemplified what I had come to admire about him. His sense of both the greatness and tragedy of human life pervaded everything he said, as did the corresponding sense that God has spoken and has given to us truth which is unshakable."

—**DAVID WELLS**, Distinguished Senior Research Professor, Gordon-Conwell Theological Seminary, Boston

"Just as there arose in the land a new Pharaoh who knew not Joseph, so the present generation risks not knowing Francis Schaeffer. This would be sad, not for nostalgic reasons, but because his thought and his work shaped a remarkable number of Christian leaders who are now developing and applying the great vision of this mentor. *Francis Schaeffer: A Mind and Heart for God* goes a long way toward overcoming this amnesia. Each author brings a moving combination of personal tributes and original insights from their own work. Few texts will give the reader deeper insight into Francis Schaeffer, the man and the legacy, than this one. And few texts will better challenge the reader to carry on the work he began."

—WILLIAM EDGAR, Professor of Apologetics, Westminster Theological Seminary, Philadephia

"Francis Schaeffer's word to the Christian community is as relevant today, and maybe more so, than in his own lifetime. No matter where you serve, no matter who you are, Francis Schaeffer has an important word for consideration as you seek to speak to a lost and dying world."

—BRUCE LITTLE, Professor of Philosophy, Southeastern Baptist Theological Seminary, Wake Forest, North Carolina

FRANCIS
SCHAEFFER

FRANCIS SCHAEFFER

A Mind and Heart for God

EDITED BY BRUCE A. LITTLE

P&R
PUBLISHING
P.O. BOX 817 • PHILLIPSBURG • NEW JERSEY 08865-0817

Library of Congress Cataloging-in-Publication Data

Francis Schaeffer : a mind and heart for God / edited by Bruce A. Little.
    p. cm.
 Conference held on the campus of Southeastern Baptist Theological Seminary, Wake Forest, N.C., Nov. 7-8, 2008.
 Includes bibliographical references.
 ISBN 978-1-59638-161-2 (pbk.)
 1. Schaeffer, Francis A. (Francis August)--Congresses. 2. Evangelicalism--History--20th century--Congresses. 3. Apologetics--History--20th century--Congresses. I. Little, Bruce A., 1945-
 BR1643.S33F725 2010
 230.092--dc22

                              2009047287

Contents

Editor's Preface

ON NOVEMBER 7–8, 2008, the L. Russ Bush Center for Faith and Culture held a conference titled, "Francis Schaeffer: A Mind and Heart for God: Engaging the Culture for Christ." This conference focused on the life and thought of Francis Schaeffer, and not on the more general work of L'Abri. In fact, I believe it is accurate to say this was the first conference about only Schaeffer, although there have been a number of conferences on L'Abri. The venue for the conference was the campus of Southeastern Baptist Theological Seminary in Wake Forest, North Carolina, location of the Center for Faith and Culture, a ministry of the seminary. The purpose of this conference was twofold: (1) to acquaint a generation of evangelicals unfamiliar with Schaeffer with his life and ministry, and (2) to consider the life and ministry of Schaeffer as a lens through which to understand how the Christian faith might engage culture in the twenty-first century.

The conference developed around the fact that American evangelicalism has been greatly influenced by the thought and ministry of Schaeffer, far more than many realize today. While some recognize the debt owed to Schaeffer, it is safe to say that for a majority of evangelicals he is only a name. Few have read Schaeffer extensively, and what many know about Schaeffer has come through secondary sources. Of course there are still those who have been influenced personally by Schaeffer and who remember his impact both on themselves and on evangelicalism in general. As author and social critic Os Guinness noted about Schaeffer: "For many in the 1960s, Francis Schaeffer was the great door opener—opening the door to regaining the lordship of Christ over the whole of life and culture. For me personally, he stood head and shoulders above most others because of the way he took God so seriously, people so seriously and truth so seriously. A flawed human being as we all are, he was a giant of the faith to whom we owe more than many people realize."[1]

In addition, the conference was more than a historical inquiry into the life and ministry of Schaeffer; it was about how Schaeffer might inform Christians in the twenty-first century on reaching culture with biblical and philosophical integrity. The conference was built on the firm conviction that Schaeffer has something important to say to those of this generation of Christians who are serious about reaching all areas of culture for Christ in a way that does more than mimic culture in order to get a hearing. Schaeffer modeled a Christ-like ministry of confronting the spirit of the age as manifest in different areas of culture without taking on the assumptions or habits of that culture. Schaeffer taught us that this requires not only a mind shaped by the Bible and trained to think critically, but a heart moved by the love of God to engage contrary worldviews with love and compassion across all of culture. Timothy George, founding dean of Beeson Divinity School, recounting Schaeffer's influence, noted: "Back in the sixties and seventies, I was one of many younger evangelicals who

---

1. This comment was given in response to a request from the L. Russ Bush Center for Faith and Culture to say something about Schaeffer as part of the promotional aspect of the conference.

fell under the spell of Francis Schaeffer. He taught us to think deeply and widely about the Christian faith, to pursue the life of the mind, and to remember the one mark of the Christian most often forgotten today—the love which lets the world know that we belong to Jesus. As never before, we need to revisit the legacy of Schaeffer today."[2] People, more than methods, were important to Schaeffer, and at the end of the day, ideas were weightier than programs. For Schaeffer, apologetics was not an intellectual game to see who could come out on top; it was a serious and compassionate intellectual engagement with people regarding the matter of truth and error, because not only truth mattered, but people mattered.[3]

Schaeffer's view of people was that they belonged to humanity—broken humanity, yes—but nonetheless humanity made in the image of God. This was more than a point of doctrine for Schaeffer; it was the ground on which he treated each person with significance and respect. David Wells, distinguished senior research professor at Gordon-Conwell Theological Seminary, recounting Schaeffer's influence on him personally, said: "One of my most vivid memories of Schaeffer was waiting for him to arrive at our small London apartment where a group of students had met to hear him speak. Schaeffer was an hour late because he had been outside in the taxi talking to the driver about the Christian gospel! But this incident exemplified what I had come to admire about him. His sense of both the greatness and tragedy of human life pervaded everything he said as did the corresponding sense that God has spoken and has given to us truth which

2. This comment was given in response to a request from the L. Russ Bush Center for Faith and Culture to say something about Schaeffer as part of the promotional aspect of the conference.

3. This point is echoed in Bryan Follis's recent book on Schaeffer: Bryan A. Follis, *Truth with Love: The Apologetics of Francis Schaeffer* (Wheaton, IL: Crossway Books, 2006).

is unshakable."[4] Reminding evangelicals, who today often seem confused about their own identity and purpose, of these ideas formed the heart of this conference.

The conference schedule consisted of four plenary sessions which concluded with a thirty-minute question-and-answer time, one address at a banquet, and a one-hour question-and-answer time with all the speakers. I believe, when you read this book, that those of you who are well-acquainted with Schaeffer and his works will be reminded of how much he has influenced your life, while those who know very little about Schaeffer will be encouraged and challenged to know more. Both, I believe, will realize how relevant Schaeffer is to the present ministry of evangelicals. At least this is the hope of the Center for Faith and Culture. Each chapter is as presented at the conference with only minor changes so as to maintain the tone and spirit of the conference. Neither the conference nor this book is intended as a promotional piece for L'Abri itself as both are about making known Schaeffer's ministry perspective and ideas that transcend time and place. The concern is how these ideas and ministry perspectives inform the work of evangelism's variety of venues and contexts whether in New York or Nigeria.

The first chapter, titled "Francis A. Schaeffer: The Man," sets forth the basic ministry perspective of Schaeffer. It is by Udo Middelmann, son-in-law of Schaeffer, president of the Francis A. Schaeffer Foundation and professor of philosophy at The King's College in New York. Middelmann explains that he is not giving a view of the personal life of Schaeffer, but of the thought of Schaeffer. This is what made Schaeffer unique in a sense (at least in twentieth-century evangelicalism), that is, his commitment

---

4. This comment was given in response to a request from the L. Russ Bush Center for Faith and Culture to say something about Schaeffer as part of the promotional aspect of the conference.

that ideas, not organizational power, are what is important in the work of the kingdom. Convinced of this, Schaeffer focused on the ideas of others as well as his own. He was not interested in hammering out a once-for-all view of everything and then going about his ministry as if he had everything figured out. His ministry was done within the context of thinking and re-thinking, since for Schaeffer intellectual honesty required that much. Middelmann, as well as the other speakers, explains how doubt played a positive role in Schaeffer's thought, not doubt of the Cartesian sort where the goal was absolute certainty, but doubt as a hedge against gullibility and groundless belief. As Middelmann points out, for Schaeffer, faith is not the starting point of life, it is the conclusion resting on the evidence. This thought is reinforced throughout the other chapters. A thought that Middelmann exposes and others affirm is that Schaeffer understood that Christianity is not merely a collection of religious ideas to debate, but that it is the truth about the universe. If Christianity is not true to this world, then it is not true at all.

The second chapter is by Jerram Barrs, resident scholar of the Francis Schaeffer Institute and professor of Christian studies and contemporary culture at Covenant Theological Seminary in St. Louis. Barrs addresses the apologetic of Francis Schaeffer in his paper titled "Francis Schaeffer: His Apologetics." He discusses three criticisms of Schaeffer's apologetic approach: (1) Schaeffer's approach was too intellectual, (2) Schaeffer made the gospel message too complicated, and (3) Schaeffer believed people could be argued into the kingdom of God. Barrs offers convincing evidence that cuts the legs out from under each criticism. Then, he addresses the question of Schaeffer's apologetic methodology. He observes how various people have categorized Schaeffer's apologetic differently, an outcome Barrs explains as a result of Schaeffer's not having one particular apologetic method. Different people focus on different aspects of Schaeffer's apologetic. For Schaeffer, the important point was to communicate the truth and not to be slavishly committed to a particular methodology—not that he was without a clear view of what he was doing and why. He began by listening carefully to the person's story and then setting about to answer the questions being asked, beginning at the point of confusion or objection, and gently moving forward to help the individual understand each step in the thought process. According to Barrs, Schaeffer, if he were classified apologetically, would probably be an integrationist of sorts. Yet, as Barrs points out, Schaeffer thought of himself as a presuppositionalist, but not in as strict a sense as the presuppositionalism of Cornelius Van Til. This chapter enlarges on and complements the first chapter, giving a clear picture of Schaeffer's ideas and ministry perspective.

Ranald Macaulay, director of Christian Heritage Cambridge, delivered the third paper, titled "Francis Schaeffer in the Twenty-First Century," on Schaeffer's unusual ability in cultural analysis, based on ideas as expressed in culture, to see where ideas were heading and what practices would logically follow. As such, many have thought of Schaeffer as sort of a prophet, not that he saw himself as such. Macaulay rehearses Schaeffer's thought regarding the development of Western culture, showing the power of ideas and the positive influence of Christianity as he places the Enlightenment as an influence contrary to the Reformation. In this vein, Ranald argues that pietism tended to rob Christianity of its intellectual muscle, resulting in Christianity's weakness in responding to the challenge of modern science. In the end, it is shown that Schaeffer, who was not a pessimist but a realist, offers real hope for the church and the world. Macaulay shows the true significance of Schaeffer for the present. It is a message to the church through the spirit of Schaeffer calling the church to a life of integrity, community, and conviction.

The fourth paper is by Jerram Barrs and is titled "Francis Schaeffer: His Legacy and His Influence on Evangelicalism." This message regarding the legacy of Francis Schaeffer was given at the conference banquet. This is a shorter chapter. Mixed with personal testimony, Barrs sets forth eight points he and others believe summarize Schaeffer's legacy to and influence on evangelicalism. It provides a succinct presentation of Schaeffer's Christian commitments, which serve as a serious call to the church today.

Dick Keyes is the director of L'Abri Fellowship in Southborough, Massachusetts, and presents the fifth and final paper, titled "Sentimentality: Significance for Apologetics." This chapter is not about Schaeffer in the direct sense, but shows how one might look at culture in Schaeffer fashion. Keyes does an outstanding job of applying Schaeffer's commitment to the fact we live in a fallen world where ideas develop that tend to be inimical to Christianity. The idea he examines in this chapter is that of sentimentality which, according to Keyes, presents the Christian with two problems: (1) if sentimentality is expressed in the Christian message, it undercuts Christian integrity in that it will gloss over the real problems of life and make Christ an "implausibility" in the public mind, and (2) when dealing with a person enamored with sentimentality there will be "built-in filters and barriers to real Christian belief," which might well obscure the real issues of life, hence making Christ unnecessary.

A final word concerning this book: it supports the belief that Francis Schaeffer's word to the Christian community is as relevant today, and maybe more so, than in his own lifetime. No matter where you serve, no matter who you are, Francis Schaeffer has an important word for consideration as you seek to speak to a lost and dying world. He never simply gave a warmed-over serving of culture's answers spiced with Christian vocabulary. He listened carefully and then encouraged people to think through the questions with him as he guided them with a Christian viewpoint. Every now and then, God gives his church a unique voice for his people—Schaeffer was such a voice. We would do well to listen, for to do otherwise would deny us that which was intended for our profit. As one among many who have been profoundly influenced by Schaeffer's ministry, it has been a great privilege to organize and be a part of this conference.

Bruce A. Little
January 16, 2009

1

Francis A. Schaeffer: The Man

UDO MIDDELMANN

IT GIVES ME much pleasure to speak to you about Francis
Schaeffer at the outset of this conference. By necessity and design,
this will have to be a limited portrait. I do not intend here to relate
to you the details of Schaeffer's biography. His birth, childhood,
family background, studies, and work have been carefully and
extensively presented. A personal and intimate record is found
in *The Tapestry*,[1] in which Edith Schaeffer has woven together
many threads into an elaborate tapestry, on which her and her
husband's fruitful life and their colorful family, past and present,
are assembled before our eyes.

Colin Duriez has recently published an excellent biography
of Dr. Schaeffer, *An Authentic Life*.[2] It is a thorough collection of insights and images from a number of researchers and
from interviews of people, members of the family and others

1. Edith Schaeffer, *The Tapestry* (Waco, TX: Word Books, 1981).
2. Colin Duriez, *An Authentic Life* (Westchester, IL: Crossway Books, 2008).

1

outside. Duriez was a student under Schaeffer in his earlier years. His biography is about Schaeffer's world of thought and practice. It also tells of the respect Schaeffer had in the eyes and ears of people outside a theological identity who had not expected Christians from a Bible-believing background to address issues of a philosophical, cultural, and political nature. Less insightful is the recent book *Francis Schaeffer and the Shaping of Evangelical America* by Barry Hankins.[3] This author appears to have only spotty familiarity with Schaeffer's world of thought and sees Schaeffer through his own presuppositions, and thereby fails to do sufficient justice to the person and his view of truth.

These doors into Schaeffer's life are available for those who wish to learn more of Schaeffer's thought and ministry. I could add minor details and personal observations: that he wrote his widowed mother a lengthy, handwritten letter before going on his day off every Monday; how he discussed Roman culture, ruins, and roads as well as current political and philosophical issues when he hiked on old trails; that he countered any blind optimism about the human race by looking at the "hair shirt" behind his bedroom curtain (in fact, he had a collage of pictures and articles by which he reminded himself of how fallen God's world really is). In this way he reminded himself of the immense cruelty of people and the brokenness of life in a fallen world. Also, I could tell you he had no time or patience for small talk; that he laughed over a few favorite existentialist jokes; and his daily prayer was that he would have neither poverty nor riches, deliberately not owning a car, staying in people's houses while on the road instead of hotels; that he gleaned ideas from any source, from books he richly underlined and annotated to

3. Barry Hankins, *Francis Schaeffer and the Shaping of Evangelical America* (Grand Rapids: Eerdmans, 2008).

articles gathered for future use in lectures and sermons. Once he used the playbill of a *Don Juan* ballet to scribble down in his characteristic handwriting thoughts that came to him during the performance. He then used the notes as the basis for a lecture on the unity and diversity within the sameness and otherness of a faithful marriage as it worked out across the many years between one man and one woman, who each change and become different at each stage.

However personal, my presentation will be, by virtue of the subject assigned to me, a focus on Francis Schaeffer as a person, to show why a considerable number of people in the church around the world look back to his life, work, and writing as the source of a more confident and even gutsy embrace of God's truth and love across all areas of life. The pleasure I have to speak to you about this is rooted in a lasting love on my part, and in an appreciation for the privilege of spending many years with him in close association and in a multitude of settings.

I first met him in September 1960, and worked closely with him for twenty-three years after completing my law and seminary studies until his death in May 1984. During eighteen of those years we were associate pastors in the International Presbyterian Church. We were also direct neighbors during much of that time (although he did not appreciate at all the barking of the dog we had collected from the pound to give it a home for a few weeks).

The first time I met Dr. Schaeffer (he had just returned from a lengthy visit to the United States to speak and for family reasons, and I had hitched a ride once again from Geneva) was a night when he was discussing with a table full of guests the view of God in theological liberalism. I remember Schaeffer saying that to the students following the view of Karl Barth and the Neoorthodox theology, there is no direct revelation from God.

3

The Bible is only a religious book, from which one may perhaps glean religious meaning in existential moments, in moments of crisis. God is for the Neoorthodox like the wind in the trees of a Chinese ink drawing: not visible, only vaguely indicated. There seems to be something there, bending the branches and moving the leaves, but in the end it is always more wishful thinking than realistic evidence. The viewer chooses to imagine the wind there, but there is no clear evidence of it.

Schaeffer had gone to Europe motivated by a burden to encourage evangelical churches and schools and people against the expanding theological weakness in the church after World War II. Higher criticism of Scripture had left the world with only a divine immanence in man and nature. This, combined with the atrocities of the war, gave rise to nihilistic existentialism and utopian ideologies, naturalistic and pagan in content. The church's response with a transcendent god of unknown characteristics could not resurrect God of the Bible. A different kingdom would now arrive on the shirttails of Darwinism, fascism, and communism without his participation. Theologians talked about God, but had excluded any direct knowledge of God. Their vocabulary attempted to give hope, but could not provide any certainty of a good God, merely a hope for a random existential experience, perhaps: a bit of wind to move the branches in a Chinese ink drawing. Schaeffer used this illustration of what became known as Neoorthodoxy: "This theology and atheism are like two bottles of poison, with the difference that the atheist bottle is marked 'poison.'"

In this situation of despair, Schaeffer proposed, as so often in later discussions and during years of sermons and lectures, that the central proposition of the Bible that God exists is more than personal views and spiritual experiences. One can speak of the truth of God's existence because the text of Scripture and the evidence of the real world give us a tightly woven net of interlocking ropes, which can carry the weight of life and answer its questions coherently. That net is held by God's hand, and he does not drop it.

Schaeffer's central contribution to the church during those years was the confident example and demonstration that the Bible is the inerrant text by which we have the only fitting understanding of the real world. That truth starts with God being there, thereby answering Sartre's basic problem: why anything exists. The infinite-personal God of the Bible is the only possible beginning of all reality, the material order of things, and the true personality of each man and woman. In a similar way, Christianity affirms our awareness of evil, horror, and death in the teaching about the historical fall of man. Consequently evil need not be denied, and while God fully knows the end from the beginning, evil is contrary to the nature of God himself and is abhorrent to him.

What I relate here about Schaeffer goes to the heart of his view of life, of God, and of man in history. I want to place particular emphasis on what was the core of his mindset, his way of thinking, and his view of reality. We shall find an honest approach, seeking answers to basic questions, questions about life and death, origins and purpose, knowledge and frustration, political authority and individual moral stands, etc. The particular way in which he approached these and other questions had a significant influence on thousands—some who met him and many more around the world who over the years only heard or read him.

This view of things for many years reached mostly individuals, and only a few at a time. Others were introduced to his view of reality through the many books he wrote and the several films he produced. He was amazed by all of this, but also saw the wider and more important result of his work when his ideas were understood, valued, and applied. He understood that they would transform the way people would see their lives and their professions when viewed in light of God and God's Word to man in the fallen world. Schaeffer really believed in the power of ideas. He thought God's Word, realistic insights, and sensible analysis shaped human belief and good actions, while bad ideas and false religions and ideologies have caused much harm and suffering around the world. According to Schaeffer, ideas shape the way man sees things. They map out a course of action and they allow us to think through alternatives without having to experience them all. When they relate to a world of facts they are helpful; when they present an ideology contrary to the facts they are deceptive, neglecting the details of real life in favor of a desirable picture that lacks concreteness and plays with our dreams in blatant disregard for the real world.

Once in a Dutch airport he was asked whether he had any weapons, to which he responded in the negative. When his case was checked and a Bible was found in it, the female guard said with a smile: "That is a weapon, isn't it?" Schaeffer loved telling this story. In his book, *The God Who Is There*, he laments that we neglect the power of modern ideas, how presuppositions shape people's worldview. He then explains their development against a background of the philosophical despair following the denial of God, truth, and reason.

When Schaeffer showed how our culture had arrived at such a place, he unlocked the door to a philosophical and not just a moral understanding of our times. With that, key evangelicals could recognize the failure of secularism and participate more intelligently in life in the public square. Schaeffer had a major part in bringing evangelicals to understand their place in the public square. He saw no need to reduce the Christian view of life to a personal relationship with Jesus independent of the wider scriptural context. The intellectual certainty of an inerrant Scripture about God, man, and history, and valuing what is right and good about human existence, were the essential components of his thinking. Schaeffer treasured what the Bible states about man made in the image of God. For him the spiritual person does not deny space/time existence, but sees it informed by God's Word, whose author is the Spirit. He taught and lived its truth, giving a high value to people even in their brokenness and encouraging them to fulfill the mandates of a life important to God and history. Sadly, that balanced view finds little room in churches, where mass is favored over mastery, where sensuality has replaced sensitivity, where religion counters but does not satisfy the mind. Sentimentality is mistaken as spirituality, and a focus on size replaces a concern for substance.

Yet Schaeffer's understanding of God's good news continues to encourage and to enliven people who apply what they have discovered for life in the marketplace and in the *polis*. His understanding is that Scripture teaches God's passion on our behalf, inviting us to live in society as family and neighbors, fully appreciating human efforts and work to do good. With the full-orbed view of life found in Scripture we can responsibly practice the lordship of Christ in different fields of endeavor, from the sciences to the arts and from the schools to the factories. It means taking ethics into economics and applying morality to humanize the market. I frequently meet people who treasure all of life more because of Schaeffer showing how sensible, coherent, and affirmative Scripture's program is concerning our existence.

Though the particulars of Schaeffer's life as pastor, philosopher, writer, and genuine human being may be less familiar today, his way of seeing God's truth is not really bound to time. He merely dusted off an older, frequently hidden perspective, which had been neglected under the effects of Gnosticism and "holiness pursuits" within the church. In fact, he loved life, including but not limited to the human body, the material world, Canova and Bellini statues, fieldstones and running water, and old roads with carefully laid edges. He liked wrinkles on a farmer's face and heavy carts to bring in the hay. After a Bible study in Lausanne, while he was waiting for the train home, he always sat with my wife (Schaeffer's daughter) for an hour or two, watching people of all ages go by and spending time talking and looking around. He liked to work with his hands. Once he even worked to move an old church building to a new location in Grove City, Pennsylvania. He saw as unscriptural the dichotomy between a fascination with the spiritual/eternal and earthly necessities and occupations. A biblical view of life has the whole man, body and spirit, rightly alive under God.

For that reason he despised death and dreaded aging, which he saw as a result of the fall. Those forms of decline he fought, and refused to accept them. He talked about his cancer as obscene, and in no way saw it as the end of his life. He read through the whole Bible once a year starting with Genesis and the creation of a material world. He did not start with the New Testament and its promise of a way to heaven. For Schaeffer, redemption was not of the soul only, but of the whole person. He understood that salvation frees us from moral guilt and from the finality of physical death. It does not, however, replace a life in the body. We still wait for that in the coming resurrection.

His view of Scripture had further ramifications. God made man in his image within an originally good creation. Our categories of understanding are accurate, because they are derived from the attributes of God. They are not adjusted for the needs of finite human beings, who then project human aspirations to the unknown beyond. The God of the Bible is not the *totaliter aliter* or "wholly other" of Kant, or Rudolf Otto in his 1917 book (German edition), *The Idea of the Holy*.[4] God does not lower himself to anthropomorphisms to adjust to our finiteness. Instead, man is addressed theomorphically; that is, the concepts and words relating to our existence have their origin in God, the creator of the real world, not man. Jesus quotes Psalm 82:6, which addresses human beings as gods, because they can understand and apply God's Word (John 10:34–36). Any continuity of categories exists from the Creator to the creature, not the other way around.

With this brief excursion from the Bible to Schaeffer's view of nature and human existence, I wanted to show how Schaeffer's insights helped the church out of its cultural ghetto. For many, he laid the intellectual foundation for wholesome relations between soul and body, mind and matter, aesthetics and ethics. For Schaeffer, Christianity is the only possible, intellectually viable explanation for all of reality.

Schaeffer taught that reality is originally a consequence of God's ideas and power. God thinks, feels, and acts: God is a person, we are told in his *25 Basic Bible Studies*.[5] Much of any cultural reality is in turn the result of the way people think, what they perceive, and how they act in the real world. "As a man thinketh in his heart so is he."[6] This is true for any person. Presuppositions about reality shape one's beliefs and practice. Out of differences grows a critique of culture; they give focus to evangelism and apologetics. Cultures anywhere are not simply God's work or composition, but the practice of good or bad

4. Rudolf Otto, *The Idea of the Holy* (Oxford: Oxford University Press, 1923).
5. Francis Schaeffer, *25 Basic Bible Studies* (Wheaton, IL: Crossway Books, 1996).
6. James Allen, *As a Man Thinketh* (1903).

ideas, of people playing either harmonious variations of God's Word and work or just a tune of their own invention out of frustration, habit, or despair.

This contrast reminds me of the first time I heard Schaeffer's voice. I had not met him yet, but listened to a recording of a discussion among students at Cambridge. The question he was answering related to God's role in history, whether all was sovereignly planned, including evil, death, and pain. Schaeffer reasoned that the universe either (1) is an impersonal everything from the beginning, without will or action or freedom, in which case all history merely takes place, unrolls, and happens according to a program; or, (2) started with a personal beginning, as the Bible teaches. In this case, history is real, and good and evil are the results of real choices for which God is not responsible. History results from free choices, and bad results follow the misuse of personal freedom.

Clive James would say it this way: "That's what history is: The story of everything that needn't have been like that."[7] Evil, pain, and death do not just exist in the flow of things, but evil results from a deliberate action of the creature against himself and against God. God's critique of history after the fall is central to the way Schaeffer, the man, saw the Christian understanding of reality. It matches each Gospel. Mark starts with the "good news" of Jesus Christ for what is a very rotten world.

The freedom to lay things out, to consider options, to debate alternatives—rather than merely to repeat positions—made Schaeffer attractive as a person. It was to him the corollary to a sentence he used on many occasions, including the conference that turned out to be his last public speaking event. He said that there is only one reason to be a Christian, and that is because it

7. Clive James, *Cultural Amnesia* (New York: W. W. Norton, 2008), 15.

is the truth of the universe. There is nothing theoretical about it. Truth was not a construct for him, but a discovery of how things hang together. They relate to each other and to the real world. The tight correspondence between text and reality confirmed the known universe, which Schaeffer described as both the universe and its form, and the mannishness of man that could only be so on the basis of the "inspirited" and not merely inspiring Scripture.

Schaeffer wanted to comprehend life in the real world. As a young man and as part of his studies for school he read through the Bible with the central questions of Greek philosophy on his mind. They had been raised and discussed in class by one of his teachers. Schaeffer wanted to know the Bible's answers to these questions before he threw it out, but didn't expect to find any. Instead, he found that the Bible not only admitted these same questions, but also provided fitting and interlacing answers. It was all like balloons tied to strings and held together in the hand of a vendor, who controlled them. Schaeffer thought he had found a previously hidden door that opens into another part of the world. The answers related to the reality of the world in which all men live.

Initially Schaeffer thought he had discovered something totally new, as the liberal church his parents attended took neither the questions nor the Bible seriously. Schaeffer was not interested in faith or religion, but came to conclude that the truth of the universe cannot hide in some mystery, but must lie before our eyes. He faced the puzzle of life, and wanted to examine and then put it together. Like a scientist, he was looking for a way to a world in which the questions lead to the answers like a shadow makes us look for the definite object. Reality presents the questions, to which only the Bible gives fitting answers. With his active and open mind, provoked by life, by people, and by all

11

of reality, Schaeffer was ready to review, reject, and recommence more than once in the quest to know the truth. This approach to life did not end when he began to believe.

The basic question was one of truth, of either cohesion or correspondence and sensible conclusions in a common field of reference. With Schaeffer's interest in engineering as his first choice of studies, the definiteness of the natural universe and the personhood of each human being were obvious sources for questions. Schaeffer found that only the Bible did justice to the way the universe is, and to questions arising out of its realities. He found that this respect for the world of data, where "life is a necessary word," is founded on God having created a world of definite things and persons. The eternal is not energy, random events, or an antecedent mystery, but a person. Later, in perhaps his most philosophical work, *He Is There and He Is Not Silent,* Schaeffer laid out this insight.

Interestingly, the starting point of his curiosity is the "here and now," the reality of things in their regularity, or lawfulness, as well as the personhood of people. Schaeffer did not start with a presupposition of belief. He did not first believe and subsequently see things in light of faith. Faith was the conclusion, not the starting point of his view of life. The reality of the world raises the questions, to which in the end only the Bible gives a framework and fitting answers. When later he talked about the need to know the presuppositions of modern culture, it is in the context of his lament over that culture's abandonment of a unified field of knowledge, an "escape from reason" indeed. He did not have in mind that people look at life from presuppositions of either faith or unbelief, but as real or unreal, true or false.

His family background had a significant influence on his respect of things and people, his later love of mountains and museums, and his interest in history and healthy discussions. In his father he saw the nobility of a day's work, the manual skills of a craft. He grieved for his mother's pain over a frustrated life, the tragic reality of disappointments, and the shallowness of hope in a world under a low ceiling. As each person inherits traits and carves out the shape of his or her own life and personality, Francis Schaeffer became interested in how people thought and acted in the world of ideas they believed, and their practical consequences. All along his life, the pursuit of truth would work around these early influences at home and the exposure to a wider intellectual world through teachers and others.

Schaeffer met the same questions about reality as a young pastor among shipyard workers in Chester, Pennsylvania, then also in the small town of Grove City, Pennsylvania, and in his third pastorate in a city church in St. Louis. He taught how only biblical Christianity gives coherent, accessible, and realistic answers for the moral and intellectual needs of each person. His interest in truth was not an interest in another world, but in this one: the world of creation, of the human condition, and of intelligent insights. He would address the people on the Delaware River front with the same teaching about God's work in history, about truth, and about how to understand it, as those in the city of St. Louis. Going from door to door, he told parents how important it was that their children attend VBS to learn from the Bible if they were to recognize and resist the bad ideas of the surrounding culture and stay out of trouble. This was no different from his later efforts when *Time* magazine called him a missionary to intellectuals.

Schaeffer's interest in philosophy, the arts, and culture did not begin with his move to Europe. It is there that it blossomed through exposure to a longer history and to people on crowded streets and markets. But already in St. Louis he would take his children every week to the art museum, ask them to sit and view

13

quietly the paintings, and then talk about them. "Which one do you like?" "Which one would you want in your room, and why?" he would ask. We see here more than a personal interest in art. He saw in art a world of ideas, struggles, and passions in the mind of the artist, directing his skill to inform and provoke people, giving insights and propositions about the real world to the viewer. Ideas, whether true or false, information or propaganda, conveying truth or deceiving with lies: ideas encourage or discourage. They weigh in and inform behavior. To have positive effects, ideas have to make sense of reality. They need to be examined by reason in light of reality. Schaeffer's interest in what the artist wanted to express enlarged Schaeffer's understanding of Christianity. In Christianity he saw better, more solidly grounded ideas to explain people in their lives and history, and how people should select the reasons and values of a good and truthful life.

For that reason, to Schaeffer, it is so beneficial to bring out the underlying ideas behind religion, politics, art, and culture generally. Evangelism must include this and then make a prayerful effort to change people's ideas on the basis of truth and reality, both of what is and what is to be avoided. As the most basic common denominator, reality does not give room to alternatives to the Bible's proposition that this is God's work and world.

If Schaeffer's interest in the arts and culture did not originate with his life in Europe, neither did his skepticism and frequent doubt have anything to do with exposure to and work among people influenced by existentialist philosophers. Schaeffer approached all things with reserved judgment, keeping his distance. He knew what unfounded enthusiasm had produced in utopian theories, in both religion and atheism. Both are no more than expressions of "faith in faith." Consequently a healthy skepticism sees doubt as wise and beneficial. It was the way his mind worked. He rejected the notion that there are "faith's reasons for knowledge." His deliberate and honest consideration of—even genuine vulnerability to—other views, his delight in open discussions without an agenda or subject, which dared his students and his own children to present alternative views of life without ever excluding any serious question, had nothing to do with a certainty of an outcome in his favor. Instead he was genuinely convinced that all knowledge in any discipline is temporary and partial. It has to be anchored better and refined more, and in that sense is "by faith." Therefore it was not inconceivable that Christianity might not be the truth of the universe, that it might then have to be rejected in the face of better arguments for something else.

What he had as an attitude, formal philosophers call the principle of theoretical falsification. Faith is not made more sure by heartfelt convictions, but by evidence. Schaeffer saw "doubting Thomas" as having done the work for us, who cannot today see the way he did back then. We are blessed, Jesus says, because Thomas also doubted for us. That doubt was removed when he could touch the risen Christ.

Belief itself is an easy thing. People readily believe all manner of gimmicks, people, and proposals. They believe diet plans, advertisements, ways to stay forever young, investment plans, and a multitude of religious claims. Belief is easy, if all you want is to believe. In this case, one belief is just as easily lost or exchanged as another. Much more complicated and rewarding is doubt, which one must never lose in the midst of a questionable human history.

For Schaeffer, this is not an arrogant doubt irrationally maintained in the face of evidence, but doubt about the finality of present conclusions, always in search of further evidence. Doubt is a way to advance, not to regress; to discover, not to

15

lose confidence; to verify, not to become cynical. Schaeffer grew through doubt, which openly admitted the challenge of God's not always obvious presence in a fallen world. He dared to raise questions to himself and others. They came in the form of uncommon propositions or troubling questions.

Jane Smiley suggests in a recent review in *The Nation* that perhaps toward the end of his life Schaeffer was less certain of what he believed.[8] But she misreads his way of alerting us to trouble on the road of life. She notices that later works had titles with a question mark: *How Should We Then Live? Whatever Happened to the Human Race?* But these are not questions as much as passionate conclusions, born from doubt about what had become social habit. They warn us, like Ezekiel before, about intellectual and moral failures.

Seeing doubt as something positive is a rather uncommon view, but it was habitually practiced by Schaeffer. An illustration may help us see the nature of that doubt: A person standing still on two legs is more stable than one balancing himself on one leg only, but the stable person never gets anywhere. Only the unstable person on one leg can begin walking somewhere. Stated in the opposite direction, Schaeffer believed that you should never jump off a cliff in fog without first ascertaining that the one who calls you is capable to deliver.

Against this background one needs to appreciate Schaeffer's willingness to start over in the quest for truth, to put all his belief aside and consider again why Christianity is true. *True Spirituality* as sermons and a book resulted from this willingness to reconsider. Schaeffer had come to see that what he had worked in for years had taken on a life of its own. It could continue in its merry ways by human instrumentation

8. Jane Smiley, "Frank Schaeffer Goes Crazy for God," *The Nation* 15 (October 15, 2007), available from *www.thenation.com/doc/20071015/smiley*.

and design alone. What would actually change if the Bible had never said anything about God's Spirit working supernaturally among his people? Schaeffer saw that much would continue the same way as before. So he resigned from his faith, church, and work to start reading his Bible, to argue for and against what he had believed, and to pray, while his prayerful and more idealistic wife was scared. But for Schaeffer it was not a matter of fear, but of integrity. Whichever way his search would turn out, it would be beneficial, for one would not want to believe that a pretend god exists, if he is really there.

These considerations were still on his mind the day he was dying. He woke up at one point and went over it again: only a personal God could explain the truth about the what, whence, and whither of life. The Greeks had no such view. Only the Bible comforts us with the propositions it gives about the real world. There exists the Infinite-Personal God whose Christ will make all things whole again.

Such a way of seeking and finding the truth of Christianity was very different from that of many of his contemporaries, who like people of faith today easily fall into a dichotomization trap. They carve out a ghetto for Christian thinking and life, teach it in their Sunday school or catechism classes, and expect it to be substantive enough to hold up under fire at the university or in daily life. But faced with opposing views, many either abandon the faith or protect their little "religion" by keeping it as something that speaks only to the home, the heart, and the church, but not to the public square.

Schaeffer had this genuine willingness and ability to doubt, to seek real answers to questions. It explains why so many were attracted to him. They came and listened for sensible answers to questions about life, for truth and meaning. He dealt with them from a love of and dependence on Scripture. He had the courage to explore both Scripture and creation as the world of grace and nature in a unified field of reference. Schaeffer reasoned against the marginalization of both Christianity and the public square from each other. Schaeffer understood the Bible to address real human beings in their functions and responsibilities on the public square. People do not abandon public concerns as Christians, and the public square remains civil, lawful, and creative only under the influence of biblical insight.

He saw neither Christians nor nonbelievers as "anthropologically other," to be kept "at arm's length." Schaeffer disagreed with the concept that it is impossible to be among the intellectual thought leaders and be a Christian. Schaeffer's love of people, wonderful and frequently odd, is related to that understanding of the one humanity. To both applies the truth of the universe in the book of God's Word, the Bible, and in the book of God's works, creation or nature. The cloth woven from real life and from the Bible's comments about real life forms tightly knit propositions about the truth of the universe: true truth, not tribal, personal, or spiritual truth.

Not surprisingly, this view is not often shared in the church. Among my teachers only one or two really understood what Schaeffer was doing as a life. Demonstrating something like reasoned persuasion to faith made him at times something of an outsider. Yet for many he was redeemed by the many who did not lose their faith and walk away from God. He spoke of "true" truth, of God actually being there, certainties which, as doctors at Mayo Clinic told him, had not been mentioned for years where they went to church. Against the trend, he insisted that Christianity is either true to the real world or not true at all. There is no use in warming the heart when the mind is not nourished and informed.

It is important also to know that Schaeffer was very much a church person. Only the church, not a particular denominational affiliation, is the bride of Christ. Perhaps for that reason he was invited to address Lutherans, Baptists, Presbyterians, Methodists, and Anglicans. He preached from the Bible about God, Jesus, and the Holy Spirit, about salvation as a matter of presenting what is true in history. It is neither an intellectual nor apologetic system, nor an appeal to emotions, but a needed understanding of what is true, real, and essential for all people to know. Any other focus would be manipulative, a way to win a game, merely a quasi-mechanical plan. Schaeffer spoke from a concern for the people in need of the important things to know, and for the God of the Bible, who wishes to be known. He saw God's grace not in exceptional, individual sovereign acts, but in his ongoing, deliberate effort to overcome the separation that sin and corruption had erected.

Starting from Scripture rather than from theology, Schaeffer presented God making every effort to get over the wall around Eden in order to reach all people with the knowledge of his existence, his character, and his passion. As Genesis 3 tells us, God is running after Adam and his descendents at all times. He sent the prophets to Israel to straighten out people's lives, came himself to Abraham for lunch, was the angel outside Jericho, was born as a babe in the manger, and returned after his resurrection to have breakfast with disciples on the shores of Galilee. He stood up from the right hand of God to welcome Stephen in his martyrdom.

On the basis of such efforts on the part of God, Schaeffer could plead and argue with each person that we must "bow, both intellectually and morally, before God" and his work. "Hurry up, but take your time," he said, encouraging both reticence before the mixed signals of a broken world, and readiness to accept what Scripture so plainly lays out for all of life in the real world. The Bible contains more about creation and redemption than the limited picture given in many churches. Schaeffer included specifically a historical fall of man and the possible return of Christ at any time in that "life in the real world" understanding. He seriously believed there to be good and sufficient reasons to believe, and could give people such time and intellectual space to find out.

Schaeffer's life work was in helping others to recognize and to enjoy the truth of the God of the Bible. The distinct emphasis was on a way of thinking and living as Christians, the confidence in God demonstrated and shared, so that people could take with them the worldview born out of the concepts taught in the Bible, use it, and apply it anywhere. Schaeffer opposed many attempts to copy his lifestyle or to focus on an expanding community. The real value lay in seeing how, in fact, the Bible does give us a reasonable, real, and accessible understanding about life without a withdrawal into religion or a fall into despair about the unfinished work of God in history.

He firmly believed that his real influence in the world would come through people understanding the ideas he set forth in his books and his films. Go and argue with them. Ideas are weightier than any expanded organizational presence. The ideas can stand on their own, while growth in numbers only contributes to dilution. As Schaeffer would encourage all: take what is available to the mind and heart and live with it in your realm, within the wonder of your calling as a human being. Power lay in the ideas, not in any association with him, back then as a person or now in his memory. His ideas shaped the efforts of an NGO relief worker I met on a dirt airstrip in northern Ethiopia. Stepping into his temporary mud hut, I saw there on a ledge books by Francis

Schaeffer that he was reading at night by the twelve-volt light he had hooked up to a truck battery.

Schaeffer's desire to focus on ideas rather than his person or an organization is also behind the lengthy discussion he had with my wife and others about a name for the study part of his work. He thoughtfully chose to name it after the French lawyer, teacher, and preacher William Farel, because few people in the wider world had ever heard of him, and there certainly was no school of thought called Farelism. Schaeffer did not want to start a movement, perhaps in part because he was burned from his earlier association with such an effort. Calvin's work in Geneva and Luther's in Germany had given names to movements, theological directions, and cultural identities. This, Schaeffer very deliberately wanted to avoid. There should be no Schaefferism, no school of thought named after him, no apologetic method, no efforts to idealize or even copy his life. He was not feigning humility in this. It came from the deep conviction that we never have "it" all together. People want the security of phrases, confessional statements and affirmations, name recognition and a leader. Sadly, the rigidity of church and state under Calvin's consistory influences many people's rejection of Christianity today in his native countries. Schaeffer's pleasure was the truth of good ideas, biblically grounded and exposed to the critique of the real world.

The simultaneous affirmation of truth and hesitation about building a systematic structure around it also reflects Schaeffer's understanding of life in other areas. He consciously resisted, for instance, the normal concentration of power that comes with a famous name or with responsibility. Repeatedly he would speak of the fact that there are "form" people and "freedom" people in organizations. Very consciously he chose to be a freedom person. He had seen the dangers of any move toward form and power earlier, and leaned against it. Rigidity of programs and forms diminishes untidy situations, but also creativity and the work of God's Spirit.

This choice to be a freedom person was carried into quite distinct areas by Schaeffer's outlook. It is interesting, for instance, that he had no master plan for ministry, no curriculum for teaching. He talked with people, preached, and lectured about things that interested him or that arose from the discussions. He also did not mentor disciples. He resisted the pressure for growth, fame, and multiplication. He prepared his material for studies, lectures, and discussions around spontaneous questions. He never copyrighted his taped lectures and sermons, because he wanted them to be available to all, but only in their totality and proper context. And finally, on several occasions he reminded everyone that he would not necessarily continue as part of his own organization if it changed. In that case, he would leave to carry on his work in other settings, for he saw his work as helping people anywhere to understand reality and their responsibility in it in light of biblical Christianity.

I experienced his being a freedom person on a personal level. Shortly before his death he urged me to extend my work and our ideas into a new area, the Christian responsibility for the poor, addressing the injustice in the world and the immorality of economic practices controlled by impersonal market forces in the hands of immoral people. His last series of sermons expounded all the passages in the Gospels that talk about money, wealth, and the responsibility for the poor, for both the body and soul. For Schaeffer, these issues of real material and moral/cultural needs arise from false ideas and result in much human suffering: false ideas about God and creation; about life and death; about authority, law, and social arrangements; about how a human being should cope in a broken world with human cruelty.

That freedom mentality encompassed his understanding of himself and his own limitations. Schaeffer hoped others would do a better job, building on his foundations. He always sought further understanding and greater wisdom. He had an open door and an open mind to entertain new insights, to study other areas of human folly and greatness. This may be difficult to follow by anyone who is tied to his ideology, whether secular or theological. They fit into their grid, never change their glasses, and therefore do not notice that reality is more complex than at first thought or that their sight has gotten worse. Schaeffer loved the challenge of people, new situations, and lively debate, no matter whether it was with Bishop Pike, university dons in Cambridge, theological students at Princeton, shipyard workers in Chester, Pennsylvania, vacation Bible school kids and their parents in St. Louis, or his own children and grandchildren.

I recall many times when he expressed his surprise after a conversation with some colleague from the past, that he was still saying the same things in the same way. "Has he never thought about anything else?" he would ask afterward. "Has he never experienced anything that would make him question his learnt responses?" Schaeffer adjusted his views when life demanded it, speculated about possibilities, wrestled with the meaning of texts, and was fascinated with what human beings do. He lived, thought, discussed, and saw new angles of view. We don't have it all together as human beings: since the fall we have been blinded by both the condition of a broken world (John 9) and sinful choices.

That leaves life mostly untidy all along, open to review, with trouble around many corners. It is the price he was willing to pay for having an open mind. Others may wish for more order to avoid unsettling confusion, but he felt that honesty about our finiteness demands an open mind, admitting piercing questions, and seeing the benefit of doubt over the whole stretch.

Jonathan Bragdon, a painter and nephew of the Schaeffers, after forty-five years still expresses his amazement that Schaeffer believed so strongly, yet was ready to throw it all out. He found that his uncle was so unusual not because he had it all figured out, but because he was prepared for constant exposure to the real world, to real people dealing with real questions. For, there are different angles to most things, and only the Bible lines them up in comprehensible and sometimes straight patterns. Here truth is not affirmation, but a conclusion, which is always open to review.

After all this you may think, as some people have suggested, that Francis Schaeffer was a pessimist, a sad person, that he could not relax, that he was intense and possibly even depressive. My impression has always been that he was more a realist, many times fully enjoying the wonder of human beings, yet always aware of the tragedy of a fallen world in so many forms. In the real world sadness looks at us in art and literature, in many faces, and in the destruction Schaeffer witnessed after the war. He was aware of the flimsy attempts to cover it all up with faith in science, progress, and money. While many content themselves for a time with these in a pleasant feeling of a quasi-religious experience, Schaeffer's reading, talking with different people, and studying history helped him never to forget a real sense of an underlying tragedy of life. His face was not that of an unhappy person, but more like one marked by genuine and generous pity for himself and others.

I believe it was this, and his attitude of doubt I explained above, that made Schaeffer such an unusual person. I see here the reason why people felt free and welcome to discuss, to argue, to think through all of life, because Schaeffer often did that himself.

He was neither shocked nor embarrassed by people's folly and brokenness, nor did he minimize what people accomplished.

That is the Schaeffer I knew, who realized that certainty comes out of the practice of doubt; that answers come mostly to people who question. Faith is easy to lose, but doubt is with us always, for we now only see as through a glass darkly. Schaeffer's distinction between true and exhaustive truth is rooted in this. For him doubt was the way to greater confidence, to a more realistic outlook; for Jane Smiley and many others it is a sign of uncertainty, of weakness, and in their overconfidence they are the more dangerous ones. Smiley writes, "The novelist in me can't refrain from seeing these titles as reflecting Francis's own doubts and uneasiness."[9]

The doubter is finally the real believer, for he is confident that he will find out, because he questions and seeks the evidence. Believers are all too easily like Job's friends. They have faith, but it was an erroneous one. They knew neither God nor the tragedy of a fallen world. They did not know Job. All they had was their nutty conviction, their poetry, their harmony of voices, and their belief: the belief that all things are fair, justice reigns, and history is the work of the will of God. No more questions. *Punkt. Schluss.*

Belief is something very dangerous. Schaeffer strongly advised against any mentality of "Just believe." He did not think that intellectual questions are that often a trick to hide moral sins. They needed to be resolved first, for it would be foolish to believe an unknown or unreliable God. Belief brought us Hitler and Stalin, and Schaeffer would probably see that list lengthened with a reference to trade deficits and huge debts, a welcome by cheering crowds in Bagdad, the Olympics in

9. Ibid., 2.

Beijing, and multiple other signs of hope and glory. People easily leave the ground of reality with too much faith, while doubt keeps us in touch with the unfinished business of wondering how to live a day at a time.

Schaeffer knew how much that goes against the popular view that one should *just* believe, whether in oneself, in Jesus, or in others. But belief alone is not enough to diminish current global warming. It does not turn ethanol into a viable fuel, nor make of Mr. Putin a friend. Belief does not release China from moral obligations to human beings in Tibetan Highlands or Darfur. Faith does not heal me; that will have to wait for either God or a handy man (or woman) with a medical license.

Schaeffer held out that Christianity is the truth of the universe and not just a Christian angle on things. He helped bind together in a biblical view of life what, until then, had been an almost random collection of denominational views, bits of life and art, a poem here and a painting there, a social effort and a prayer time, a sermon about salvation, and a doctor's struggle against death. He helped bring together the concern for the soul and body of man, explaining the meaning of life in a moral framework of historical Christianity. Dust had covered the biblical view of life and work for some time. When it was blown away, the beauty and wholeness of a fuller life under God became visible again to a generation, and many have found it a great privilege and pleasure now to live more responsibly in that world.

2

Francis Schaeffer: His Apologetics

JERRAM BARRS

FRANCIS SCHAEFFER said himself that the heart of his apologetics can be found in the three books, *The God Who Is There, Escape from Reason,* and *He Is There and He Is Not Silent.* These three books together set forth an outline of Schaeffer's apologetic approach and how he defended and commended the truth of Christianity. *Escape from Reason* and *The God Who Is There* are primarily an analysis and response to the dominant ideas in Western thought and culture. *He Is There and He Is Not Silent* also deals with many of the ideas set forward today as alternatives to historical biblical Christianity, but also presents a basic Christian worldview in a more systematic way than do the other two books. Other summaries of his apologetic approach can be found in *Whatever Happened to the Human Race? How Should We Then Live? Death in the City,* and *Genesis in Space and Time,* and by audio in many of the lectures that are still

27

available on tape through L'Abri and from the tape ministry Sound Word.[1]

A lecture series that stands behind *He Is There and He is Not Silent* is titled *Possible Answers to Basic Philosophical Questions*,[2] which is an example of Schaeffer's apologetic method put into practice. These lectures were given several times during the 1960s at L'Abri in Switzerland, where I first heard them. He also gave them as a set of special lectures at Covenant Theological Seminary in St. Louis, Missouri, when he came as a visiting lecturer while I was a student there between the years of 1968 and 1971. I remember the lectures very well as I took them for one hour of seminary credit, and consequently took thorough notes (which I still possess). In fact, I have them before me as I write this.

But the primary reason I remember the lectures so well is that the lectures were open to the public (although they were not widely advertised), and all through the week a handful of visitors would join us in the tiny seminary chapel. I remember one man, an unbeliever, who came faithfully to the whole week of lectures. Schaeffer covered the three areas of existence, morals, and knowledge, and showed how in each of these areas "modern man"—or his term, "modern-modern man" (today he would say "postmodern man")—is left only with the hell of alienation. Christianity, on the other hand, gives answers in each of these areas, answers that are satisfying both intellectually and personally. At the end of the week he finished by saying that with the Christian answer there can be true beauty in each of these three areas. The young man who had attended so faithfully became a Christian as the last lecture finished.

1. See, for example, a basic lecture titled "Apologetics," found at http://www.soundword.com/l-abri-schaeffer--francis.html.

2. Available from Soundword.com: http://www.soundword.com/l-abri-schaeffer--francis-possible-answers-to-basic-philosophical-questions---part-1.html.

I mention this story here, both because it is a precious memory and also because it reveals something about the way Schaeffer approached his lecturing and his writing. The title of the lectures, *Possible Answers to Basic Philosophical Questions,* probably sounds abstract for many when they first come across it. Schaeffer, however, was not interested in either abstract or purely academic apologetics. He was an evangelist—that is how he thought of himself and how he spoke of his ministry.

Those particular lectures, all the other lectures he gave, and all of his apologetic books were developed to answer the questions of both Christians and non-Christians who came and sat at his table in Huemoz-sur-Ollon in Switzerland, the village where he and Edith had founded the work of L'Abri. I personally know many people who became Christians listening to his lectures, either when the lectures were originally given, or when they listened to them on tapes as they studied at L'Abri or in other settings all over the world. He would use the same approach that can be found in his lectures and books when he discussed the truth of Christianity with unbelievers or doubting Christians at mealtimes (as Edith served delicious food to meet their other needs). Or, if the weather was good, as he sat on the bench outside their chalet and talked with visitors to L'Abri, he would urge them to consider the truth claims of the gospel using the same approach. Or, as he walked through the forests, fields, and mountains of that lovely part of Switzerland, he would encourage his companions to raise their questions and doubts about the Christian faith and he would give answers to their questions.

Francis Schaeffer believed passionately that Christianity is the truth about the universe in which we live. God is indeed there, and he is not silent. God, he would say, is not an idea projected from our minds, or from our longings, onto the giant screen of the heavens, a kind of superhuman created to meet our needs. God is not a thought in the system of a philosopher who cannot cope with having no answers to the dilemmas of our human existence. No, God truly exists, and he has spoken to us in the Bible to tell us about himself, about ourselves, and about our world. He has made known to us what we could never discover by ourselves in our questioning and searching.

God has revealed to us the truth about the world in which we live, the truth about our human existence, and the truth about himself. He has spoken this truth to us in his Word, and therefore the message of the Bible fits with the nature of reality as we experience it. To use an image, the biblical account of human life fits like a glove on the hand of reality. Christianity is true to the way things are. Schaeffer was deeply convinced of this, and indeed every believer should be convinced of this. When we stand up in a worship service and declare the affirmations of the Apostles' Creed, we are saying what we believe to be true:

> I believe in God, the Father Almighty, Maker of heaven and
>   earth;
> And in Jesus Christ, His only Son, Our Lord
> Who was conceived by the Holy Ghost,
> Born of the Virgin Mary,
> Suffered under Pontius Pilate;
> Was crucified, dead and buried . . .
> The third day he rose again from the dead,
> And ascended into heaven.[3]

These affirmations are not like cartoon balloons floating loose in the air. No, they are statements about the way things truly

3. William Barclay, *The Apostles' Creed* (Louisville: Westminster/John Knox, 1983), 1.

are. The Christian is saying: "This is the truth about the world, about God, about history."

Schaeffer often used to say: "I am more sure of God's existence than I am of my own!" That may sound a little strange or extreme, but he was simply acknowledging that if God did not exist, then we would not exist. His existence is prior to ours in time, of course, but also prior to ours as he is our Creator. Human life is possible only because the Christian triune God lives. In the same way God's moral perfection is prior to our understanding of morality. God's character has always been one of holiness, goodness, and justice. It is because God is good that we can affirm that there is a difference between good and evil. It is because God is good that we can commit ourselves to the pursuit of moral beauty. Morals are possible for us because God is moral.

In the same way God's love is prior to our love. The members of the Trinity have loved each other for all eternity, from "before the beginning" as Schaeffer used to say. Because we are made in the image of our Creator, we are designed to love, designed for relationships—a relationship of love with our Creator and relationships of love with one another. Love is possible for us because God is love. I remember a wonderful wedding sermon he preached from John chapter 17 titled "Before the Beginning." In this sermon he spoke of the eternal reality of love and communication between the members of the Trinity as the sure foundation for all human relationships.[4]

Furthermore, God's knowledge is prior to our knowledge. God knows all things truly—indeed he knows all things "exhaustively" as Schaeffer would say. We humans are created by God to have knowledge: knowledge about the Lord, knowledge about

---

4. See his sermon "Before the Beginning" available from Soundword.com: http://www.soundword.com/l-abri-schaeffer—francis-before-the-beginning.html.

ourselves, and knowledge about our world. We will never know exhaustively, for we are finite, but we can know truly; otherwise, we would not be able to function at all in this world. Even despite our fallenness we can still have true knowledge because of God's commitment to care for us and for all creation, and because of his kindness in granting his wisdom to the whole human race. Knowledge is possible for us because God knows all things and because he upholds all things, and he has designed us so that there is coherence between us and everything around us. Because we know God, or rather, because God has made himself known to us, it is possible for us to know ourselves. Calvin said, "It is certain that man never achieves a clear knowledge of himself unless he has first looked upon God's face."[5] Schaeffer's statement, "I am more sure of God's existence than I am of my own," is very similar—we can only know ourselves truly when we come to know God.

Whereas Christianity is the truth about the world in which we live and about our lives, it is proper for Christian believers to encourage one another, to encourage our children, and to encourage unbelievers to ask their questions, to express their doubts, and to raise their objections against Christianity. We do not need to say to the doubting Christian or to the unbeliever, "Don't ask questions—just believe!" We do not need to say when a Christian has struggles and uncertainties about his faith: "Just pray harder!" Schaeffer would say, "If you try to load every doubt, objection and question on the donkey of devotion—eventually the donkey will lie down and

5. "Accordingly, the knowledge of ourselves not only arouses us to seek God, but also, as it were, leads us by the hand to find him. Again, it is certain that man never achieves a clear knowledge of himself unless he has first looked upon God's face, and then descends from contemplating him to scrutinize himself." John Calvin, *Institutes of the Christian Religion*, ed. John T. McNeill, trans. Ford Lewis Battles, vol. 1 (Philadelphia: Westminster, 1960), 1.1.1–2.

die, for it is being asked to bear a load God never intended it to bear."

God has made himself known in his Word in such a way that we can think carefully about what he tells us. That is why, said Schaeffer, the Reformers were so eager to get the Bible translated and into the hands of all the people—so that they could read God's Word for themselves. In addition, God has made himself known in the created order and in human nature in such a way that we can think carefully about what he has revealed. What God says is "true and reasonable"—to quote the apostle Paul when he was defending the message of the gospel—and it is not "done in a corner" (Acts 26:24–29).

In the same way the apostle Peter encourages Christians always to be prepared to give a reasoned defense of their hope in Christ (1 Peter 3:15–16). Schaeffer saw this calling to be able to give a reasoned defense as part of the birthright of every believer—not just of pastors or some specially trained apologists. He was terribly distressed when people would come to his home at the point of giving up their faith because no one in their church would take their questions seriously or because they would be rebuked for asking questions or expressing doubt.

I remember one young woman who came to L'Abri filled with pain because of the response of her parents when she raised questions about the Christian message. Her father was a pastor, but as a young teenager she began to have doubts and she wrote down some of her doubts and questions in her personal journal. One day her mother started reading through this journal (although it was private) and was horrified to read there the struggles her daughter was having. She shared the journal with her husband and they threw her out of her home, declaring that she must be "reprobate" because of the doubts she had expressed. She was then just sixteen years old!

This is an extreme example, but all of us who worked in L'Abri with Schaeffer could share many horror stories such as this. This kind of situation broke his heart, and he would devote himself to listening for hours to the struggles and questions of those who came to his home. He would say: "If I have only an hour with someone, I will spend the first fifty-five minutes asking questions and finding out what is troubling their heart and mind, and then in the last five minutes I will share something of the truth." I am often asked: "What about Schaeffer made the greatest impression on you?" I think all of us who had the privilege of working with Schaeffer would respond to such a question: "His compassion for people."

Some who came to the Schaeffers' home were believers struggling with doubts and deep hurts such as the girl above. Some were people lost and wandering in the wasteland of twentieth-century Western intellectual thought. Some had experimented with psychedelic drugs or with religious ideas and practices that were damaging their lives. Some were so wounded and bitter because of their treatment by churches, or because of the sorrows of their lives, that their questions were hostile and they would come seeking to attack and to discredit Christianity. But, no matter who they were, or how they spoke, Schaeffer would be filled with compassion for them. He would treat them with respect, he would take their questions seriously (even if he had heard the same question a thousand times before), and he would answer them gently. Always he would pray for them and seek to challenge them with the truth. But this challenge was never given aggressively. He would say to us (and he would model for us): "Always leave someone with a corner to retire gracefully into. You are not trying to win an argument, or to knock someone down. You are seeking to win a person, a person made in the image of God. This is not about your winning; it is not about your ego. If that is your approach all you will do is arouse their pride and make it more difficult for them to hear what you have to say."

Schaeffer believed and practiced the conviction that it is God who saves people. Indeed, he would frequently encourage people to leave L'Abri for a time and to go off by themselves to think through what they were hearing. He would say that we do not have to try to push and to pressure people into the kingdom. He loved the words of the apostle Paul: "We have renounced secret and shameful ways; we do not use deception, nor do we distort the word of God. On the contrary, by setting forth the truth plainly we commend ourselves to every man's conscience in the sight of God" (2 Cor. 4:2). Because Christianity is true, and because God is the one who delights to draw people to faith in Christ, we do not need to put emotional pressure on unbelievers, nor do we need to try to manipulate them into responding to our message. Rather we commend the truth to them by seeking to show them that it is indeed the truth, and we pray for the Spirit to open their hearts to that truth.

In addition to his deep compassion for people in their struggles and in their lost state, Schaeffer also had a strong sense of the dignity of all people. The conviction that all human persons are the image of God was not simply a theoretical theological affirmation for him, nor was it just a wonderful truth to be used in apologetic discussion. It was a passionate shout of his heart, a song of delighted praise on his lips, just as for David in Psalm 8:4–5:

> What is man that you are mindful of him,
>   the son of man that you care for him?
> You made him a little lower than the heavenly beings
>   and crowned him with glory and honor.

The truth that we are the image of God, a truth that is at the heart of all his apologetic work, was, for Schaeffer, a reason to worship God. This conviction of the innate dignity of all human persons had many consequences for Schaeffer. He believed, and he practiced the belief, that there are no little people. He invited people into his home who were damaged in body and mind and he treated them with the same dignity and compassion as the most brilliant or accomplished visitors. He was just as willing to spend time with the maid or the janitor in a hotel as he was to go and talk to someone considered "important" in the eyes of the world or of the church. He took a conversation with one damaged and needy young person as seriously as when he was talking with the president or lecturing before an audience of thousands.[6]

This same conviction of the dignity of people and his compassion for them led him to avoid aggressive confrontations with unbelievers. His refusal to "debate" with anyone, including a radical liberal such as Bishop Pike, was an example of this. He insisted that their meeting should be called a "dialogue." Those who attended that "dialogue" said the most impressive part of it was that it was evident Schaeffer could have demolished Pike's positions and his arguments and made him look foolish and extreme—but he did not. What was evident was his compassion for this man and his commitment to treat him with dignity. One friend shared with me how he went up to talk to Schaeffer after the public meeting was over. When he arrived behind the stage Schaeffer was surrounded by people eager to congratulate him and to ask him questions, but Bishop Pike was standing by himself on the other side. When Schaeffer realized this, he politely excused himself from his questioners and went over

6. See Francis A. Schaeffer, "No Little People, No Little Places," in *The Complete Works of Francis A. Schaeffer*, vol. 3 (Westchester, IL: Crossway, 1982).

to talk to Pike. As a consequence of this occasion they became friends and corresponded with each other until Pike's death while he was searching for manuscripts in the desert.

This conviction of the dignity of all people also led Francis and Edith into their work of child evangelism. To the Schaeffers, children were just as significant as adults, just as precious, just as worthy of receiving our time and effort. In "The Secret of Power and the Enjoyment of the Lord"[7] he wrote, "There is a certain gentleness about really great Christians. There are many ways to observe this, but perhaps one of the best is to notice the tenderness for children in some of the great warriors of the past." While living in St. Louis as a pastor in the middle years of the 1940s, Edith and he started a ministry to children called Children for Christ.

This work eventually became international and was greatly used by God to reach many children with the gospel. Edith and he wrote the materials for the meetings, and Edith designed flannel graphs to be used with them. These materials were translated into many languages, and he and Edith traveled extensively teaching others how to lead children's meetings. They would model this by leading a study with the adults as if they were a group of children. If one is able to find a copy of these materials (there were, for example, studies on Genesis and on the Gospel of Luke—the latter published in a different format under the title *Everybody Can Know*), it quickly becomes clear that Schaeffer takes the same basic approach to communicating biblical truth to children as he does with adults. I had the privilege of leading an evangelistic study for inner-city children while I was a seminary student in St. Louis, and managed to

7. This is a two-part article published in consecutive weeks during 1951. See Francis A. Schaeffer, "The Secret of Power and the Enjoyment of the Lord," *The Sunday School Times*, July 1 and July 8 (1951): 539–40; 555–56.

find a copy of the studies on Genesis to use in my teaching. The study was, in essence, a beginner's version of *Possible Answers to Basic Philosophical Questions* and of *Genesis in Space and Time*, and I found it very helpful in communicating God's truth to those young African-American city dwellers.

Obviously in this context the communication of truth to children is taking place with the use of different language and with other appropriate adjustments, but children need precisely the same truth and ask just the same questions. In fact, some of the most difficult questions I have ever been asked were from little children. In these Bible studies for children the Schaeffers were dealing with the same fundamental questions about the nature of human existence and with the same wonderful answers that the Bible gives to these questions—the very same questions and answers that he presents in *He Is There and He Is Not Silent*. This is an important point to notice for several reasons. First, Schaeffer was sometimes criticized for being too intellectual. Some have said that he was dealing with issues that "ordinary people" don't wrestle with in the course of regular life. The fact that the same questions and truths could be used (and used very powerfully, and in a way that was greatly blessed by the Lord) to communicate the good news to little children shows the inappropriateness of such a criticism of his apologetic work. Second, in similar fashion Schaeffer was accused of making the gospel too complicated. Why did he not simply tell people the ABC of the gospel? You are a sinner, Christ died for you, now repent and believe in him.

His response was that all people (including little children) have to understand and respond to the truths of the biblical worldview, and to turn from their idols and from whatever false ideas they have put in place of God's truth. They have to believe "that [God] exists" (Heb.11:6) and to accept the truth of who God is and who they are as human persons before they can understand that they are sinners and that Christ died for them. If people already share a Christian worldview because of growing up with a church background and with knowledge of the Bible, then, of course, we may begin with the ABC of the gospel, for then the ABC of the gospel will make sense to them. But, if they are like the people of Athens whom Paul addresses (Acts 17:16–34), then we will have to start with the true nature of God and with the false ideas and idolatry of the pagan thinkers, if we desire to make Christ known to them.

Schaeffer recognized that there are fewer and fewer people who truly hold to a biblical worldview. Consequently he saw that it is absolutely essential with the majority of people we meet to begin at the beginning. The beginning for modern people, and even more for postmodern people, is denial or doubt about the existence of God and denial or doubt about the existence of truth. While these might seem like abstract issues, they are not in fact abstract. Rather, they are very practical. Nothing is more practical, nothing is more basic, than the conviction that there is truth that can be known. Without this conviction, life becomes more and more intolerable and more and more filled with alienation. The more consistently people live with the loss of truth, the more their lives will fall apart, for the center does not hold.

A second response that should be made to this criticism— that he was making the simple gospel too complicated—is that he did not develop his apologetic approach in a study far removed from the lives of real people. He developed the answers he gives in all his apologetic writings and lectures in the heat of battle, so to speak. His home was filled with people seeking answers to the questions of existence, morals, and knowledge.

I worked for almost twenty years in L'Abri, many of those while Francis Schaeffer was still alive. Our pattern was to tell those who came to our homes that "no questions are off limits." For if we believe that Christianity is indeed the truth, we do not need to be afraid of any questions or objections. Consequently, almost all the lectures that were given were given in response to the questions, doubts, and struggles of those staying with us. The issues addressed in Schaeffer's apologetic works are the questions of real people.

My own conversion bears on this issue. As a non-Christian I wrestled with several of the problems that are addressed repeatedly by Schaeffer. I wondered how any meaning and value can be given to human life. "Who am I, and is there any ultimate meaning to my life?" were questions that plagued my soul. I did not see any basis for being able to make a distinction between good and evil. I felt there was a difference, and I longed for there to be a difference, but I could find no reason for such a difference. Does not the same end come to those who seem morally upright and those who devote themselves to wickedness? Does it ultimately matter, or is it just an illusion to think that moral integrity is important? I was haunted by the reality of suffering. Is there any reason for suffering, any ultimate explanation for it, or is it meaningless in the end? Is it just that we live and die, we win some and lose some, we have fleeting moments of joy and longer periods of sorrow, but none of it makes any sense? And is there any resolution to suffering? Or do we simply have to endure it, either with passive resignation or bitter rage—as Dylan Thomas urged us: to "rage against the dying of the light"?[8]

8. Dylan Thomas says, "Do not go gentle into that good night, Old age should burn and rave at close of day; Rage, rage against the dying of the light." See Dylan Thomas, "Do not go gentle into that good night," in *The Poems of Dylan Thomas* (New York: New Directions Publishing, 2003), 239.

When I was a teenager growing up in England in the sixties many of my friends struggled with such questions, but most of them attempted to drown their anxious thoughts with alcohol, drugs, or promiscuous sexual encounters, or to bury themselves in trying to find a life that would give them "personal peace and affluence" (to use Schaeffer's expression). I found myself unwilling to take either of these routes, for both seemed a betrayal of everything I treasured (largely thanks to my parents, who were truly good people and who were excellent parents with a genuinely happy marriage). For me, the lack of answers drove me to the very edge of suicide. I was prevented (Thank God!) from throwing myself over a cliff one January day by the glory of creation even in the middle of winter. I felt constrained to keep searching just a little longer before taking such a final step.

About two weeks after this I met a Canadian, Mike Tymchak, a doctoral student at Manchester University where I was an undergraduate. He had studied under Francis Schaeffer at the Swiss L'Abri and had discussions, Bible studies, and sessions listening to Schaeffer's tapes in his apartment each week. The first of these evening meetings that I attended after I met Mike, he led a reading and reflection on the first two chapters of Ecclesiastes. It pierced me to the heart, for here was a man, Mike, and here was a book, the Bible, that took my questions seriously and began to give me answers. Over the next months Mike played tapes by Francis Schaeffer that covered some of the ground retraced in the book *He Is There and He Is Not Silent* and in other of his basic apologetic books and lectures on tape. Mike's own approach to my questions was the approach that Schaeffer took. Within a little over a year and a half, Mike led me in a prayer of commitment one Tuesday evening in November 1966 as we knelt side by side on his kitchen floor. God had brought another reluctant sinner to himself!

41

A third criticism that is sometimes made of Schaeffer's apologetic approach is that he believed he could argue people into the kingdom of God. Nothing could be farther from the truth. He stated categorically many times that argument alone will not save people. He did not acknowledge this because the reasons that demonstrate the truth of Christianity are inadequate. They are not inadequate; rather, they are fully sufficient to persuade an open-minded person. People, however, are not open-minded. We are all rebels against God, with wills resistant to his truth. Schaeffer would say, as he says in several of his lectures, that to come to the truth men and women have to bow before God three times. We have to bow as creatures, acknowledging that God is God and that we are not the source and origin of our own life. Rather, we are dependent. Our hearts resist this. We have to bow morally, acknowledging that we are to see God as the lawgiver, that we are people who consistently have disobeyed his commandments, and that we deserve his judgment. We are dependent utterly on his mercy in Jesus Christ. Finally, we have to bow in the area of knowledge. God is the source of truth and we are not. We are dependent on him in order to understand the world and even our own existence.

In addition to this recognition of the problem of the hard heart, Schaeffer understood that there are three elements, all equally important, to the demonstration of the truth of Christianity: persuasion, life, and prayer. This understanding was not merely theoretical. His life's work was built around the practice of three elements. One, we are called by God to make his truth known, and to demonstrate that truth to unbelievers, by giving them compelling reasons for faith. These reasons are found in God's own revelation in Scripture and in creation. They are not the clever inventions of our minds. Schaeffer believed his apologetic method was faithful to Scripture and that he was using the approach of Scripture. Two, we are called by God to live the truth, to demonstrate the truth of the gospel by our lives. Schaeffer called the life of the Christian "our final apologetic" and sought to show in his own life, "in some poor way" as he put it, the reality of "supernaturally restored relationships." He believed the New Testament teaches us that the non-Christian ought to be able to see a difference in our lives and thereby draw conclusions about the truth of the message of Christ that we proclaim. Three, we are called by God to pray that he would demonstrate his existence in the reality of his answers to our prayers. Francis and Edith Schaeffer prayed that God would bring to L'Abri the people in whose hearts he was at work. Schaeffer knew, and constantly repeated to those who worked with him, that the work of saving people is impossible for us, but it is indeed possible for God. He was a man of prayer who humbly believed that without the work of God in the hearts and minds of people, all our labors are in vain.

Actually, I ought to have set these three points in the reverse order, for Francis Schaeffer believed, and spent his life practicing the belief, that prayer is the most important work that we do whether in the task of apologetics or in any other area of our Christian obedience. In one sense he would say: "Prayer is an activity that must be central to our lives," but then he would quickly add: "In prayer we are holding out the empty hands of faith to the God who is there and who can do far more abundantly than all that we ask or imagine!"

Where did Francis Schaeffer fit in the classification of different apologetic methodologies? Robert Reymond declared that Schaeffer was a Classical, or what he calls an "empirical apologist."[9] Classical apologetics seeks to demonstrate God's

9. Robert L. Reymond, *The Justification of Knowledge* (Darlington: Evangelical Press, 1984), 145–46.

existence and theism as the only correct worldview to believe. This demonstration is given through the use of the "theistic arguments" (made famous by Thomas Aquinas), and is then followed by appeal to historical evidence to establish other important matters, such as the deity of Christ, his historical resurrection, and the reliability of Scripture. Proponents of this view are usually said to include Anselm, Aquinas, William Paley, B. B. Warfield, R. C. Sproul, Norman Geisler, John Gerstner, and J. P. Moreland.

Gordon Lewis thought Schaeffer was a Verificationalist, or someone who holds to what is called Cumulative Case Apologetics.[10] This approach suggests that the truth of the Christian message is not strictly a formal argument to "prove" Christianity, or an argument from probability. According to Steven Cowan, "It is more like the brief that a lawyer makes in a court of law or that a literary critic makes for a particular interpretation of a book. It is an informal argument that pieces together several lines of data into a sort of hypothesis or theory that comprehensively explains that data and does so better than any alternative hypothesis."[11] Those who use this approach are usually said to include Basil Mitchell, C. S. Lewis, C. Stephen Evans, and Paul Feinberg. Feinberg writes: "Christian theorists are arguing that [Christianity] makes better sense of all the evidence available than does any other alternative worldview on offer, whether that alternative is some other theistic view or atheism."[12] On this approach the Christian account of reality given to us in Scripture explains such foundational matters as the existence and

10. Gordon R. Lewis, "Schaeffer's Apologetic Method," in *Reflections on Francis Schaeffer*, ed. Ronald W. Ruegsegger (Grand Rapids: Zondervan, 1986), 71.

11. Steven B. Cowan, "Introduction," in *Five Views on Apologetics*, ed. Stephen B. Cowan (Grand Rapids: Zondervan, 2000), 18.

12. Paul D. Feinberg, "Cumulative Case Apologetics," in *Five Views on Apologetics*, ed. Stephen B. Cowan (Grand Rapids: Zondervan, 2000), 152.

form of the cosmos, the nature of morality, religious experience, historical facts such as the virgin birth and resurrection of Jesus, and the hope of ultimate redemption.

I think Francis Schaeffer would have been fascinated to have seen these attempts to pigeonhole him into a particular approach. But where did he think he fit in the usual classification of: Classical Apologetics, Evidential Apologetics, Verificationalism, Presuppositionalism, Reformed Epistemology Apologetics, and Fideism? Schaeffer regarded himself as a Presuppositionalist, although he sometimes resisted the attempt of others to put him in any particular category. Presuppositionalists stress the deep impact of sin on every aspect of our humanity, including our knowing. Because of this, they argue that the unbeliever has to be challenged at a more foundational level than a presentation of powerful evidence for the truth of the Christian message. This position recognizes that every human person has assumptions, or presuppositions, that shape everything the person believes and the way that person lives. Because we are fallen away from our original state of innocence and live in rebellion against our Creator, not one of us starts our investigation of the world, of human life, and most especially of God, from a place of neutrality. The unbeliever has a heart turned away from God toward idols, especially the idol of the self, and this precommitment of the heart stands in the way of hearing and receiving the truth. The Christian apologist should gladly acknowledge his or her presupposition of the truth of Christianity. God exists and he has spoken—this is the starting point of apologetics. Evidences and arguments may be marshaled to support the truth claims of Christianity, but at base the apologist argues that all morality, all meaning, all rationality presupposes the existence of the God who has made himself known in Scripture. "We should present the biblical God, not merely as the conclusion to an

argument, but as the one who makes argument possible."[13]
Schaeffer would have been in thorough agreement with this
statement of John Frame.

While Francis Schaeffer saw himself as a Presuppositionalist, and he would have affirmed the outline of the approach to
apologetics that I have set out above, he is not easy to fit into
a box, and this is why he has been classified in other ways by
Reymond and Lewis. This is also the reason why he was criticized repeatedly by Van Til as being inconsistent to a properly
presuppositional approach to apologetics. Part of the challenge
here is that rather than developing a particular methodological
approach, Schaeffer had a passion for the communication of
Christian truth both to believers and to unbelievers, and he
was very gifted at this task, whether he was speaking to people
who considered themselves intellectuals, or to ordinary working people without much book-learning, or to little children.
He very carefully said that he was not an academic apologist,
but rather an evangelist. He would always add that he was not
implying that academic apologetics was an inappropriate calling,
but it was not his calling.

He also was, from his earliest years, passionately committed
to seeing the common ground of different perspectives among
believers, including the common ground of differing apologetic
approaches.[14] One of the earliest articles Schaeffer wrote was an
attempt to get J. Oliver Buswell, a leading Classical apologist,
and Cornelius Van Til, a Presuppositionalist, to see that they had
much in common. Schaeffer's article was written in response to

13. John M. Frame, "Presuppositional Apologetics," in *Five Views on Apologetics*,
ed. Stephen B. Cowan (Grand Rapids: Zondervan, 2000), 220.

14. For an excellent treatment of Schaeffer as an apologist "who favors integration"
between different apologetic methods, see Kenneth D. Boa and Robert M. Bowman
Jr., *Faith Has Its Reasons: An Integrative Approach to Defending Christianity* (Devon,
England: Paternoster, 2006), 425–82.

a series of exchanges between Buswell and Van Til, exchanges that had become fairly heated and which had troubled some of the readers of the magazine in which they had been printed because of the lack of charity that seemed to be creeping into this to-and-fro. Schaeffer, then a young man of 36, urged the two to recognize that they both believed that reasoning alone could not save anyone, that both insisted people are rebels trapped in sin, and that both admitted gladly that without the work of the Holy Spirit in the heart and mind no one would come to faith. He urged them to acknowledge they both agreed that only God's Word makes sense of human life. In this article Schaeffer set forth an outline of his approach to apologetics that helps us understand his life's work. I will summarize what he wrote in my own words, as a series of brief points:

1. All people, no matter what their beliefs or way of life, live in God's universe, for it is the only one there is.

2. The unbeliever may indeed invent another world to inhabit, a world of false gods, idols, a world where there is an obstinate refusal to worship and serve the true God and Maker of all things. Such an invention is what all religions and alternative worldviews are—not truth but a kind of make-believe.

3. His invention does not fit what is truly there—so the unbeliever lives between two worlds, worshiping and serving the gods he or she has chosen, but living in actuality in the world that God has made.

4. If the unbeliever were consistent to his or her make-believe world, then he/she would be driven to meaninglessness, amorality, and irrationality. But, thank God, no one is fully consistent.

5. The unbeliever has to live in deceit, benefiting from God's world and the beneficence of his general grace but suppressing the truth in unrighteousness.

6. God constantly confronts the unbeliever with the truth, for the Spirit is the world's prosecutor. He both gives people up to the consequences of false ways of seeing the world they have chosen to serve, and also continues to pour out his good gifts on the unbeliever. These gifts are a testimony that challenges the unbeliever to repent and seek the one true God, and they render the unbeliever inexcusable.

7. We are to focus on the tension, helping the unbeliever to see that all that is good and true and beautiful comes from God and that God's world and gifts are his true home, while also exposing the inadequacy of the worldview or idol to which the unbeliever has given mind and heart.

8. We are to remember that we are never consistent either, in our thinking or in our lives, for we as believers are all still living in two worlds; therefore, understanding our own fallibility and inconsistency, we are to communicate the truth with humility, understanding, grace and respect.[15]

Another way to summarize how Schaeffer approached the task of making truth known to people would be to say that he used presuppositions as a kind of evidence. We may imagine him speaking like this, while all the time praying for the Holy Spirit to open a person's heart and mind: "If you turn away from God and make a world of your own imagining—there will be terrible

15. See Francis A. Schaeffer, "A Review of a Review," *The Bible Today*, October (1948): 7–9.

consequences, both for the way you think and for the way you live. Yet at the same time because you live in God's world and you are made in his image you will be restrained from being consistent to your way of seeing the world. (Schaeffer would speak very often of these two realities, "the universe and its form and the mannishness of man," acting as a constraint on people's thinking and their lives.) If, on the other hand, you would turn to the Lord you will find the world 'falling into place' in your thinking and your life will be set free by the truth."

Schaeffer saw his work as simply applying Paul's words in Romans 1:18–32, where Paul sets out the consequences of suppressing the knowledge of God and of worshiping and serving part of the creation in God's place. Another way to put this would be to say that Schaeffer's approach was similar to Isaiah's in Isaiah 40–48, where the prophet contrasts the folly of the worship of idols with the wonder of the worship of God, and sets out the consequences of these two ways of thinking and living. In Psalm 115 we see the Psalmist doing precisely the same thing when he sings of the glory of the Lord and contrasts that with the emptiness of idols and the way they make those who worship them become like them. False belief systems, just like practical idolatries, destroy our humanity. Only the truth made known by the triune God can makes sense of our lives and set us free to be truly human. This was Schaeffer's passionate conviction. He spent his life defending this conviction and seeking to bring others to acknowledge the Lord who graciously gave us the truth and who sets us free as we bow to him.

3

Francis Schaeffer in the Twenty-First Century

RANALD MACAULAY

A TWENTIETH-CENTURY PROPHET?

If I heard Francis Schaeffer say it once I heard him say it a thousand times, "I am no prophet." Yet many still find this the most natural way to describe him. In fact, it is increasingly the case as we enter the twenty-first century, probably for the same reason we find ourselves here at this conference. People constantly say, "Schaeffer is more relevant today than a quarter of a century ago when he died." Take for example the opening paragraph of his final chapter in *How Should We Then Live?*: "Overwhelming pressures are being brought to bear on people who have no absolutes, but only the impoverished values of personal peace and prosperity. The pressures are progressively preparing modern people to accept a manipulative authoritarian government. Unhappily, many of these pressures are upon us now."[1]

1. Francis A. Schaeffer, *The Complete Works of Francis Schaeffer*, vol. 5, *How Should We Then Live?* (Wheaton, IL: Crossway, 1982), 245.

First and foremost in Schaeffer's list of these pressures is "economic breakdown." "At a certain point," he says, "economic breakdown seems all too possible." Then come the pressures of "war or the serious threat of war," "the chaos of violence including indiscriminate terrorism," the growing disparity between wealth and poverty in the world (with the corollary of wealth redistribution), and the "growing shortage of food and natural resources in the world."[2]

With the financial meltdown going on around us, Schaeffer's relevance is obvious. Yet this is not all. Step by step, he outlines the logic and inevitability of the West's demise and, therefore, what may await us. In his view there can be only two alternatives, either a return to the Christian faith or growing centralized control:

> If these pressures do continue to mount, which seems probable, do you think people . . . will, at great cost to themselves, . . . stand up for liberty and for the individual? Countries that have never had a Christian Reformation base will be the first to bow to authoritarianism. Already a growing number in Asia and Africa have gone this way. Men in Western governments . . . did not understand that freedom without chaos is not a magic formula which can be implanted anywhere. Rather, being modern men, it was their view that because the human race had evolved to a certain point by some such year as 1950, democracy could be planted anywhere from outside (sic). They had carefully closed their eyes to the fact that freedom without chaos had come forth from a Christian base. They did not understand that freedom from chaos could not be separated from its roots.[3]

He then reaches back exactly seventy years to "a disquieting memory" when social fragmentation in Germany led to mounting

2. Ibid., 245–47.
3. Ibid., 249.

control and tyranny. It is as bleak an image as any during that brutal century: the British prime minister, Neville Chamberlain, emerging from the door of his aircraft with a copy of the Munich Pact dated September 30, 1938. He then utters the now almost unbelievable words of self-deception, "Peace in our time!" to which Winston Churchill responds with characteristic bluntness and accuracy:

> [The people] should know that we have sustained a defeat without a war. . . . They should know that we have passed an awful milestone in our history . . . and that the terrible words have for the time being been pronounced against the Western democracies: "Thou art weighed in the balance and found wanting." And do not suppose this is the end. This is only the beginning of the reckoning. This is only the first sip, the first foretaste of a bitter cup which will be proffered to us year by year unless, by a supreme recovery of moral health and martial vigor, we arise again and take our stand for freedom as in the olden times.[4]

Schaeffer quotes this, of course, to underscore the fact that danger remained also in 1976. Now, thirty years later and with the banking crisis particularly in mind, the same alarm echoes around the world and nowhere more insistently than in the United States. It is at least possible that an even more "awful milestone" than 1938 has recently been passed.[5]

4. Ibid., 249–50.
5. Schaeffer's final exhortation in relation to the dangers he anticipates in the twenty-first century deserves to be quoted in full: "We are not excused from speaking (i.e., against the special sickness and threat of our age—the rise of authoritarian government) just because the culture and society no longer rest as much as they once did on Christian thinking. Moreover, Christians do not need to be in the majority in order to influence society. But we must be realistic. John the Baptist raised his voice . . . and it cost him his head. . . . Here is a sentence to memorize: 'To make no decision in regard to the growth of authoritarian government is already a decision for it.'" Ibid., 256.

At this point in his book, Schaeffer has completed a survey of Western civilization from the first century on. A brief postscript called *A Special Note* is then given, primarily for Christians, in which he closes with the watchman analogy from Ezekiel 33. The watchman is commissioned to alert the city as danger approaches. If he fulfils his responsibility and the city fails to respond, he bears no guilt. If, on the other hand, he fails to alert the city, the guilt of all who perish remains on him. Whereupon Ezekiel has the people cry out, "How then should we live?" (Schaeffer's book title), and Ezekiel quickly responds in God's name: "I have no pleasure in the death of the wicked; but that the wicked turn from his way and live" (Ezek. 33:10–11, KJV).[6] So, even within sight of disaster, hope remains. Ezekiel and Schaeffer know well that the living God of the Bible whose nature is always to have mercy is Savior as well as Lord and Judge.

That Schaeffer chooses to bring his message to a close in this way is striking. With Daniel on one side and Ezekiel on the other it provides a fitting ending. Not that he implies any identification with them, of course. Yet their breadth of national and even international concern finds an unmistakable echo which makes his prophetic ministry almost unique in recent history. Like Churchill, he acted as a watchman to the Western world and warned of approaching danger, simply because the facts demand it. He eschewed being called a prophet, but perhaps that is what he was.

THE PROPHETIC ANALOGY

The analogy lends itself to four preliminary observations. First, thinking of our title, "Francis Schaeffer in the Twenty-First

6. Ibid., 257.

Century," we naturally want to know what Schaeffer might have said if he were here now. An element of conjecture remains, of course, for history has moved on. But our introduction thus far serves to show how prescient he was, and limits the degree of uncertainty. He "saw" the future, so to speak, and spelled things out pretty clearly. So the major part of what remains in this paper tries to elucidate that message.

Second, with respect to Churchill's reference to Belshazzar's feast in Daniel 5, we find a helpful foreshadowing of contemporary Western perfidy, with one important difference. While feasting with his thousand friends and concubines, Belshazzar defies God. He calls for the gold and silver goblets reserved for worship in the temple at Jerusalem and carouses with them as he worships his idols. Suddenly a hand writes on the wall and the fateful words "MENE, MENE, TEKEL, UPHARSIN," appear (Dan. 5:25). He has been weighed by God and found wanting. That very night he dies. The image of moral waywardness and stupidity fits well with our contemporary hubris. The culture is saturated with consumer greed and ridicules the Judeo-Christian God meanwhile. In this it resembles Belshazzar's idolatry. Yet the Babylonian king made no claim to follow Jerusalem's God. In this sense he was a complete outsider to the Judeo-Christian tradition. By contrast, our Western society descends lineally from that very source. One wonders, then, what awaits the West.

Given that Schaeffer was prophetic, our next question to ask is how much evangelicals paid attention to his message. In Britain, initial interest and enthusiasm quickly gave way to neglect bordering on aversion. For many reasons British evangelicals took exception to Schaeffer: he was too clear, too fundamentalist, too outspoken, too confusing, too simple, too demanding, too confrontational. The result was that his books, from having been best sellers, quickly dried up. Finally I was approached by the publishers to see whether we could rescue them from being pulped, and thousands ended up in an attic at the English L'Abri where I worked. The interest in the United States, by contrast, was widespread and sustained. Many realized the significance of what Schaeffer was saying, particularly in the areas of theology, philosophy, and the public square. In all three, his ideas proved seminal in reference to biblical authority and inerrancy, to art, to apologetics, and to public debate, for example. The growth of "worldview" literature in the States is another indication of his influence. As for his lead in sanctity-of-life issues, the response was out of all proportion to anything in Europe including the United Kingdom, complicated as it was in certain respects as we shall see. Nevertheless, relative to what was actually needed, the response was weaker than it might have been. His teaching on "true spirituality" influenced some but not many. His insistence that churches should be real communities rather than "preaching points" seemed to go unheeded. And the model of community living that he sacrificially demonstrated within the L'Abri Fellowship remained virtually incomprehensible to American audiences.

Finally, to the criticism that Schaeffer's prophetic warnings were too pessimistic, the context of his wider ministry, particularly toward the end of his life, gives us a different perspective. Around the mid-1970s he deliberately chose to restrict his speaking engagements to the United States. He felt that if American evangelicalism could be renewed and reformed, the nation as a whole might be turned around. He decided that that was the window of opportunity in which he should participate. The American church's numerical strength and Bible-believing tradition made it unique. Nowhere was there potential like this—scores of Christian colleges and seminaries, vast numbers attending church, dozens of publishing houses committed to biblical theology and culture, innumerable parachurch organizations and media channels engaged in public debate.

Although his more public ministry began in England—*Escape from Reason* and *The God Who Is There* appearing there first—he decided by the late 70s to concentrate on the American church. For those of us based in the United Kingdom it was a costly decision, for his ongoing presence might well have made a difference. But he really did think the American church could give the lead to its increasingly rudderless society and thereby influence the world. Whether or not he was right in this is another matter. Either way, his aspirations *vis a vis* the United States show how positive he actually was. He continued to warn, but his warnings came from a yearning, not a hopeless heart. And if in his final book and accompanying United States tour, *The Great Evangelical Disaster*, he sounds a further lament, he is expressing sadness not despair.

Added to that, it has to be remembered that he was not alone in raising the alarm. Carl Henry for example saw clearly the way things were going and wrote of his fears, if anything more starkly than Schaeffer. And clearly he was no pessimist: "We may even now," he said, "be living in the half-generation before all hell breaks loose—and we will be remembered, if we are remembered at all, as those who gave their hearts and minds and very bodies to plug the dykes against impending doom!"[7]

EVANGELICAL OPPORTUNITY

But Schaeffer knew better than most that the culture's collapse meant greater opportunity for the church. By the time he

7. Carl F. H. Henry, *Twilight of a Great Civilization* (Wheaton, IL: Crossway, 1988), 181–82.

finished *How Should We Then Live?* he had already chronicled the "line of despair" coming out of the Enlightenment. "Matter plus time plus chance," he repeatedly said, "cannot result in personality and meaning." But this was what our intellectual leaders had left us with by the time he wrote. Later, Richard Dawkins would say it boldly: "In a universe of blind physical forces . . . some . . . are going to get hurt and (others) are going to get lucky and you won't find any rhyme or reason in it, nor any justice. . . . There is at bottom no design, no purpose, no evil and no good, nothing but blind pitiless indifference. . . ."[8] How could a universe comprised only of matter provide succor for the most deeply treasured ideals of the human heart—love, justice, goodness, beauty, and compassion? Schaeffer saw the futility involved and pressed home the obvious solution, which was that the West needed to return to its roots.

With this in mind it is striking to see Niall Ferguson's recent attempt to deal with the problem of Western vacuity. In an attention-grabbing headline in 2005 he blurts out: "Heaven Knows How We'll Rekindle Our Religion, But I Believe We Must."[9] He fears equally the rise of Islamic terrorism and New Age irrationalism. But within his own humanistic framework he has nowhere to turn: "The decline of Christianity—not just in Britain but right across Europe—stands out as one of the most remarkable phenomena of our times,"[10] he says. Why? Because of the "moral vacuum our de-Christianisation has created," which has simply "delivered us into the hands of others' fanaticism. . . ."[11] So he suggests a weekly dose of churchgoing,

8. David Robertson, *The Dawkins Letters* (Fearn, Rosshire: Christian Focus Publications, 2007), 92.

9. Niall Ferguson, "Heaven Knows How We'll Rekindle Our Religion, But I Believe We Must," *The Sunday Telegraph*, July 31, 2005.

10. Ibid.

11. Ibid.

boring though the sermons and singing might be. This would at least "help to provide an ethical framework for your life. And I certainly do not know where else you are going to get one."[12]

It would be laughable were it not so pathetic—a leading Western intellectual, a professor at both Oxford and Harvard, wistfully scratching about in the ashes of his culture's past to resolve a quandary of his own making. His "hard-shelled materialist" philosophy, as Schaeffer has been saying, goes nowhere. But the problem was obvious already a long time ago. As early as 1835 De Tocqueville emphasized that America's unique freedom and prosperity could survive only if it maintained its original vision. He writes, "If the members of a community as they become more equal become more ignorant and coarse, it is difficult to foresee to what pitch of stupid excesses their selfishness may lead them."[13]

At which point the true poignancy of our current evangelical predicament begins to surface. The culture's intellectual and moral bankruptcy provides unparalleled opportunities for the church. Its vacuum needs to be filled—and indeed will be filled—by whoever provides the most cogent lead. The gospel really is the power of God unto salvation, and evangelicals could and should be giving that lead. Yet they are patently ill prepared.

EVANGELICAL COMPLEXITY

The development of evangelicalism in the Western context is not a simple matter. There are a number of forces, both

12. Ibid.

13. Alexis de Tocqueville, *Democracy in America*, vol. 2, trans. H. Reeve and ed. Phillips Bradley (New York: Knopf, 1945), 124.

internal and external, influencing the shape of evangelicalism. Schaeffer recognized this complexity.

Historical Background

Understanding present situations requires a grasp of the historical context from which evangelicalism emerged. Schaeffer understood the force of ideas that turned him to consider the development and flow of ideas.

Freedom without chaos. Schaeffer's view is that in the early 1500s, a new society takes shape in Europe based on the Reformation principles of *sola scriptura*, *sola fide*, and *sola gratia*. Here, the law of God is an unvarying, universal, and heavenly measure by which both nations and individuals are finally judged. Nothing changes immediately in Europe, yet the benefits of this religious shift steadily appear. The logic of the Reformation continues through the Puritan "revolution" of the seventeenth century and serves to illustrate Schaeffer's theme that only the Bible can provide a proper balance between form and freedom in society, where "freedom" avoids becoming anarchic, and "form" avoids becoming oppressive. Age-old traditions are thus challenged. Medieval religious authority and superstition are repudiated. The divine right of kings is questioned. The English Civil War of 1642 ensures that the first shoots of parliamentary government and the rule of law begin to sprout, albeit tentatively. The Commonwealth gives place to the Stuart Restoration (1660), and that in turn to the "bloodless revolution" (1688) which provides needed stability but at the expense of the reforming vision: political power is concentrated in the hands of a small oligarchy; the Puritan revolution is stopped in its tracks; those identified with it are excluded from university and public office.

Nevertheless, the core values of the new political structure survive and later bear fruit.

Meanwhile, the Mayflower settlement of 1620 and the far larger emigration under John Winthrop in 1630—with John Harvard its best-known member—ensure that the sixteenth-century ideals are more clearly evident in New England. In due course the United States comes into being and develops into the largest, freest, and richest democracy the world has ever known. Not that any of this is what it should be, either in the United Kingdom or in the New World. Confusion and controversy mount. Battle lines are drawn. Petty rulers act as much from greed as from religious conviction. Europe is engulfed in war. The Americans import slaves and ride roughshod over the Indian natives. Nothing is ideal. No "golden age" emerges either then or subsequently. Yet the Reformation and Puritan societies bear favorable scrutiny when measured alongside alternatives elsewhere in the world. As John Roberts puts it in his magisterial survey of Western culture:

At the deepest level it is in its Christian nature that the explanation of medieval society in shaping the future must lie . . . . At (its) heart lay always the concept of the supreme, infinite value of the individual soul. This was the tap-root of respect for the individual in the here-and-now . . . (and) its importance can easily be sensed by considering the absence in other great cultures—Islam, Hindu India, China—of such an emphasis. In none of them was the safeguarding of individual rights to be given much attention until the coming of Western ideas.[14]

It is an emphasis familiar in Schaeffer's thought: freedom without chaos comes only from a Christian base. He clearly means

14. John Roberts, *Triumph of the West* (London: BBC, 1985), 108.

"Protestant-Christian" here, for the Counter-Reformation in Spain, Portugal, Italy, and France led elsewhere. Hence John Roberts's earlier qualification when outlining the renewal principle inherent within any Christian society: ". . . its search to change the world and its self-criticism, ensured that medieval civilization never lost the capacity for self-renewal . . . though that renewal was only achieved . . . in the Reformation."[15]

Modern science. But Schaeffer goes farther and shows that modern science, like liberal democracy, also had its roots within a Christian worldview. Modern science begins *before* the Enlightenment and, therefore, is a Christian rather than a humanist invention. The single greatest influence in shaping the scientific method is the biblical worldview, whether Catholic or Protestant, as Rodney Stark illustrates helpfully in his book *For the Glory of God*.[16] The empirical method of modern science is as foreign to alternative worldviews as constitutional democracy.

This clarifies one of Schaeffer's main themes: what was gained by the Reformation was placed in jeopardy by the Enlightenment. As the humanist influence (the Enlightenment) gathers momentum it causes a shift, jeopardizing what the Reformation had achieved (freedom without chaos). Finally, only the economic momentum generated over centuries of Western growth and prosperity holds everything together (an outcome of the biblical worldview), but for how long? Western affluence masks an inherent instability. We return to where we began with Schaeffer's insistence that freedom *with* chaos leads inevitably to breakdown.

15. Ibid.
16. Rodney Stark, *For the Glory of God* (Princeton: Princeton University Press, 2004), 121.

Evangelistic Ironies

At this point three ironies about contemporary evangelicalism awkwardly confront us. From the early 1800s, evangelical churches in the West committed themselves to ever more strenuous programs of evangelism. But as they did so, their own culture slipped farther and farther from its original faith. They were successful elsewhere in Asia, Africa, and South America. The gospel spread dramatically and the universal church was enriched as a result. At the same time, however, all seemed to no avail at home. Clearly something was missing.

Although, too, the entire edifice of Western civilization arose from Christianity's inherent dynamic, intellectually (as much as morally) evangelical churches in the West neglected and in some cases even disowned their intellectual heritage. According to Mark Noll, "From the perspective of 1930 the evangelical mind in America was nearly dead. . . . Not only were the nation's universities alien territory for evangelicals, but (the fundamentalists) had made a virtue of their alienation from the world of learned culture."[17] As a result the intellectual citadels of the West remain firmly secular—and no wonder given the "scandal of the evangelical mind."

Finally, as has been said, given the level of intellectual and moral disarray outlined by Niall Ferguson, the potential for change is apparent. Yet evangelicals seem to be unable to capitalize on this and are often unaware of the virtual collapse of the humanist mind. Lack of a Christian mind leaves them defensive and exposed. They lack the apostle Paul's confident appeal to the non-Christian culture of his day, on one hand unashamedly proclaiming the gospel and on the other spending time trying to

17. Mark Noll, *The Scandal of the Evangelical Mind* (Grand Rapids: Eerdmans, 1995), 211.

persuade people that the message was true—a fertile combination of proclamation and persuasion. Even today, however, one hears it said that proclamation is all that matters, that to argue is to rely upon "human philosophy," and to debate and confront intellectually is to overlook the power of the "simple gospel." It is, of course, an unnecessary and unbiblical antithesis and it cripples the church. Yet much of the evangelical community limps forward like a one-legged veteran on crutches, desperately trying to "reach the culture" yet failing because it has neglected one whole aspect of the apostolic model.

What then would Schaeffer say to all this? How would he explain the curious phenomenon of a Christian culture severed from its religious roots while the church looked on? Why is evangelicalism today powerless to redeem the situation? It is a complex question, but I think he would have traced much of the blame to the twin ailments that we call "the Pietist Hangover" and "the Virus of Technique"—the first involving the loss of a Christian mind, the second the ready acceptance of consumer values and techniques within the life of the church.

The Pietist Hangover

We are now in a better position to understand Schaeffer's true significance for the present. The Reformation principle of total engagement in society had, by the mid-nineteenth century, been transformed into cultural and political disengagement, although, of course, with notable exceptions on both sides of the Atlantic.

The earlier view is well represented by Martin Bucer: "The purpose of the Reformation," he says, "is 'to restore, establish and strengthen the administration of religion and of the whole republic according to the word of Christ our Saviour and supreme King.'"[18] His key words are "and of the whole republic." Immediately we are returned to what we considered earlier of both England and New England. Richard Hofstadter notes: "In its inception New England was not an agricultural community, nor a manufacturing community, nor a trading community: it was a *thinking* community, an arena and mart for ideas, its characteristic organ being not the hand nor the heart but the brain. . . . Theirs was a social structure with its cornerstone resting on a book."[19] Hence, as he goes on to say, the New Englanders immediately founded a university.

By the time we reach 1859, however, the atmosphere is different. Darwin's *Origin of Species* is published and C. H. Spurgeon preaches his "Revival Year Sermons." Thousands flock to hear him, but the evangelicals are in fact on the edge of a cliff and about to fall off. By 1918 the church as a whole is in free fall. What has intervened since the Reformation is the Pietist renewal beginning in Germany around 1700 and carried far and wide by converts such as the Wesley brothers. Jacob Spener, a Lutheran minister, spearheaded a much-needed critique of dead orthodoxy. A short essay of his titled "Disideria Pietatis" (pious desires), written in 1675, sold widely. Many were awakened by it and by the simpler Bible-centered preaching Spener promoted. They deliberately met together in small "collegia" or assemblies. Out of these came a movement which spread rapidly through Europe and across to North America. Missionaries even made their way to India. The problem, however, was that the encouragement of "heartfelt religion" tended to displace the importance

18. Martin Bucer, "De Regno Christi," in *Melanchthon and Bucer*, ed. Wilhelm Pauck, trans. Wilhelm Pauck (Philadelphia: Westminster), 155–73.

19. Richard Hofstadter, *Anti-Intellectualism in American Life* (New York: Vintage, 1966), 59.

of intellectual conviction. Equally, private godliness became the focus of attention rather than involvement in culture. Little by little a new ethos emerged favoring "heart" over "head" and "private" over "public."

Had this happened at another time it might have been less serious. But this was the eighteenth century. The Enlightenment was challenging Christianity to the core. It co-opted modern science and claimed that scientific knowledge was more reliable than "faith." Several of the Founding Fathers in the newly formed American republic made no bones about revising the ancient creeds. Thomas Jefferson, for example, supplied a reworked edition of the story of Jesus where he concludes that Jesus was a good man, whose moral teaching deserves attention, but certainly not a miracle worker or a divine Son of God! At about the same time Percy Bysshe Shelley was being expelled from Oxford for writing on "The Necessity of Atheism." Humanism was on the march, and the intellectual battle joined. Meanwhile, the American frontiers were quickly moving west. Rural church ministries were less easy to maintain than those in the cities. Methodist circuit riders were commissioned to take the gospel to the settler communities. Invariably they were less educated than their East Coast equivalents. Periodic revival meetings had to suffice. The message needed to be simple and the focus sharp: "conversion" and "experience." It was the Pietist agenda.

Tragically, when the Christian mind was most needed it was virtually absent. As Hofstadter says, "From 1875 to his death in 1899 Moody was not only the unchallenged leader of a new phase in American evangelism but the greatest figure in American Protestantism. . . . The knowledge, the culture, the science of his time meant nothing to [him] and when he touched upon them at all it was with a note as acid as he was ever likely to strike. In this respect he held true to the dominant evangelical tradition."[20] Christian leaders such as Spurgeon were bewildered by "the downgrade controversy" which questioned the historicity of both Old and New Testaments. Some evangelicals held their own, but in the main it was a rout. Seen in this light, Schaeffer's ability not merely to understand the new intellectual climate but to engage meaningfully with it is impressive. When he first received public attention in England in 1967 it caused shockwaves through the evangelical community. Here was someone who was uncompromisingly "conservative" in doctrine, yet conversant with contemporary culture and able to expose its pretensions. Some would argue, however, that evangelicalism had already turned its back on Pietism by this time. This is partly true. Carl Henry, Billy Graham, and others in the United States, along with their counterparts in the United Kingdom, had recognized the need for change. Important steps had been taken. The intellectual commitments essential for re-engagement had already been framed and these were later enshrined in the Lausanne Covenant of 1974. Evangelicalism worldwide *had* moved on.

But Schaeffer provided something unique even then. What many evangelical churches at the close of the Second World War represented was a type of ghetto culture. The philosophical issues lying behind the rapid changes of the 1950s and 1960s were a closed book to them, so they lacked the background with which to capitalize on what he was giving them. While rallying to the call for action, especially in issues such as abortion, they were unable to engage meaningfully in the larger discussions. They often came across as single-issued and shrill. Even their best responses to Schaeffer tended to be theoretical.

20. Ibid., 107.

Apologetics became a new interest but rarely extended beyond their evangelical communities. What he aimed at was to make the gospel relevant to the non-Christian world. Theoretical apologetics were of little interest to him. His goal was to take the gospel to the opposition on its own ground, more "street fighter" than academic, more "evangelist" than "philosopher" or "theologian." But he was one of a kind. Later, evangelical colleges began to take responsibility for this area and to equip the next generation for public debate, and much has changed as a result.

The "hangover," however, continues to exert a stronger influence than is often realized. Some of this relates to the "Virus of Technique," which comes next. But most of it, I suggest, goes back to Pietism's almost indelible stain within the system. Even today evangelical leaders overlook the central issue of the twentieth century, what Schaeffer called "true truth." Preachers, for example, who otherwise repudiate Pietism and insist on an intellectually rigorous exposition of the Bible, fail to equip their hearers adequately. They quite rightly emphasize the centrality of God's Word and the unchanging nature of creedal statements from the past, but leave the ideas of the culture unchallenged. So believers lack confidence intellectually when they most need it. They learn doctrine, but not how to use it in the contemporary discussions about truth and plausibility. Among their colleagues and peers they remain defensive. They hear the Bible preached faithfully, but in an intellectual vacuum, not as prophetic confrontation. Reformation preaching, by contrast, took issue with the intellectual ideas of the day, especially with medieval theology in the Roman Catholic Church. They strove to take "every thought captive to the obedience of Christ" (2 Cor. 10:5). It was what Schaeffer longed to see *vis a vis* the modern world, but even now he is rarely imitated in evangelical pulpits either side of the Atlantic.

At the opposite end of the spectrum lie the preachers who identify more or less with the emerging church. Being rightly sensitive to the inadequate response of most "conservative" churches, they are keen to explore alternatives—to make their churches more community oriented, more flexible, more human, less critical of differing lifestyles, less politically stereotyped, and so on. I think Schaeffer would have been sympathetic to their aspirations for the same reason he was eager to accept the hippies of the 1960s and 1970s into his home in L'Abri. Where he would have parted company with them, however, would have been in their rejection of "propositional truth." To him this would have represented a disastrous compromise with the spirit of the age. As he said in his "Special Note" at the close of *How Should We Then Live?*: "Let us remember the hallmark of the present generation of humanistic thinking. It is the acceptance of the dichotomy between meaning/value and the area of reason . . . that is, existential methodology."[21] Not that Schaeffer would ever have suggested that truth is conveyed only in propositions. Human life involves so much more than propositions, and Scripture itself speaks in a variety of forms reflecting that variety and richness of human experience—and not least narrative. But the moment evangelicals surrender the primacy of propositional revelation, all is lost.[22]

The Virus of Technique

As if it were not already serious enough for mid-nineteenth-century evangelicalism to have lost a Christian mind, another even

21. Schaeffer, *Complete Works*, vol. 5, 253.
22. R. Albert Mohler, "Truth and Contemporary Culture," in *Whatever Happened to Truth*, ed. Andreas Köstenberger (Wheaton, IL: Crossway, 2005), 53.

more serious affliction struck. The Industrial Revolution was already well advanced by that time. New technologies were being spawned by the decade, each in turn eagerly welcomed as a means of social and individual benefit. Science was not merely a theoretical tool, it was practical; it could literally "produce the goods." Modern technology introduced a "brave new world," but it was as difficult a world for evangelicals to cope with as the world of ideas had been. Sadly, all too few realized what was happening. Indeed, the entire culture seemed to be overwhelmed. As Morris Berman puts it, "One could argue that corporate consumer culture is tantamount to a kind of nuclear attack on the human mind. . . ."[23] The deception lay in the mind-set induced. Development and progress came to be viewed almost exclusively as science-based advances. Social improvement could best be effected, it was supposed, not by right ideas and moral discipline but by scientific method. Whole new "sciences" were spawned on this premise: sociology, psychology, economics. Social improvement meant finding the right technique. Frederick Taylor's *Principles of Scientific Management* (1911) became a significant turning point, according to Neil Postman.[24]

Already in the first half of the nineteenth century, American evangelists had accommodated themselves to this new methodology. Calvin Colton wrote in 1832 that revivals were "matters of calculation by the arithmetic (sic) of faith in God's arrangements. Formerly a visitation of the Spirit was unexpected and apparently unasked," he said, ". . . now it is the divine blessing upon measures concerted by men and executed by men, where the instruments are obvious."[25] John Kent says a similar thing about Charles Finney's

23. Morris Berman, *The Twilight of American Culture* (New York: Norton, 2000), 96.
24. Neil Postman, *Technopoly: The Surrender of Culture to Technology* (New York: Vintage Books, 1992), 51.
25. Calvin Colton, *History & Character of American Revivals* (1832); quoted in John Kent, *Holding the Fort* (Norwich: Epworth, 1978), 18.

new way of doing things: "Between 1800 and 1860 the professional revivalist was an American phenomenon. . . . He was the inventor of *new techniques*. . . ."[26] Placed side by side with our earlier quote about Moody's lack of interest in culture, the mixture becomes toxic. Techniques were not inappropriate in and of themselves, of course. Nineteenth-century evangelists were not wrong to plan, any more than they were misguided in using modern technology. Neither implied lack of dependence upon God. But the subtlety of the problem obscured its danger. What tended to get squeezed out were God's priorities for Christian experience. The nineteenth-century evangelists were symptomatic of a later disease which, more than a century and a half later, proved lethal.

Schaeffer understood the danger. Soon after meeting him in Cambridge in 1958, I recall him saying that he felt American churches promoted the gospel and ran their affairs "the way big business sells cornflakes." A new formula now prevailed: no longer was it a case of finding *personal* solutions for practical problems; now it was a case of problems of all sorts, whether personal or mechanical, requiring the right *program*. The prayerful, the personal, and the non-mechanical—all were in danger of being pushed aside by market forces and "organization." In fact, though it sounds surprising given his influence in ethics and apologetics, this issue became a central, if not *the* central, focus of Schaeffer's ministry after 1950. The individual believer is summoned first and foremost to "a moment-by-moment relationship with the living Christ"—not to techniques of evangelism or church growth or anything else. He or she is to imitate Christ, to share in his suffering and become like him in his death—what he called being "rejected, slain and raised."[27] It was an emphasis on the personal as over against the mechanical, the simple

26. Ibid.
27. Francis A. Schaeffer, *True Spirituality* (London: Hodder & Stoughton, 1971), 38–39.

and insecure as over against the efficient and powerful. Clearly this was his core passion. If he addressed it less directly than others, such as David Wells for example, his introduction to *True Spirituality* places it beyond doubt. This was the book, he said, which should by rights have appeared first, for he had worked on it before the foundation of L'Abri in 1955. The apologetic work came later.

Edith Schaeffer's *The L'Abri Story* is important at this point. The Schaeffers had been expelled from Switzerland for their "Protestant" impact upon a Catholic village in the canton of Valais. What happened to them and their family was completely unplanned. It wasn't anyone's Big Idea. There was no plan to reach Europe for Christ, no program for planting churches, good as both of those might have been. No wealthy donors or skillful fund-raisers waited in the wings. Certainly Schaeffer had no idea of becoming a "Billy Graham to intellectuals" as *Time* magazine described him. Yet this tiny seed became, under God, a major influence in late-twentieth-century evangelicalism. The sheer impossibility and strangeness of it all was enough to encourage Schaeffer to break completely from the all-too-common model he had come from. He had questioned it already but L'Abri gave him the environment in which to demonstrate his new direction. Not that he or the work ever suggested this model should be copied. That wasn't the point. L'Abri began without requests for money, co-workers, or visitors/students, even without a plan—a principle continued to this day throughout the eight communities worldwide.[28] Schaeffer was insistent that Scripture demanded none of these four things. What concerned him was the need to break loose from an increasingly impersonal culture in both church and society.

For all its theological orthodoxy, this is what he saw the evangelical church to have become by default. In this respect everything

28. See www.labri.org.

he wrote and did was a protest against the "Virus of Technique." He couldn't have spelled it out more clearly. It saturated his books on the church, *The Church at the End of the 20th Century*, *True Spirituality*, and *The Mark of a Christian* in particular. He longed to see prayer and genuine community given their rightful place in the local church—all made possible on the basis of the power of the Holy Spirit and consecrated service. Yet few seemed to pay any attention. Even among those who welcomed his work on apologetics it remained a blind spot. The virus had desensitized his audience enough to make him unintelligible.

CONCLUSION

The fact that this Schaeffer conference has taken place at all gives grounds not merely for thanksgiving but for hope. A new Schaeffer biography called *An Authentic Life* (2008) is a further indication that his life and teaching have not been forgotten. We also know what he would have said had he been with us now, as I have tried to show. Western culture has sown the wind and is now reaping the whirlwind. But nothing in history is inevitable. Human beings, not machines, are what create it. Change is always possible. What then if evangelicals, as the rightful heirs of those who founded the civilization, were to arise and recover their true identity? It would require a miracle, of course, as at the Reformation. Only God's kindness and intervention could make it happen. And Christians would need to take account of their earlier mistakes. The "Pietist Hangover" and everything related to it would have to be rooted out and intellectual confidence restored. Worship of God would need to be seen in terms of involvement in the whole of life. Real communities would need to be established and the "Virus of Technique" taken in hand.

One thing, however, would be uniform. The church would need to look very different from what it does now. As David Wells puts it: "the Church (must begin) to form itself . . . into *an outcropping of counter-cultural spirituality.* . . . It must give up self-cultivation for surrender; entertainment for worship; intuition for truth; slick marketing for authentic witness; success for faithfulness; power for humility; a God bought on cheap terms for the God who calls us to costly obedience. It must in short be willing to do God's business on God's terms."[29] This was precisely Schaeffer's burden. It was the heart of his prophetic vision for the church in the twenty-first century, and my simple alliteration below is an attempt to fix it in our minds. Simple as it is, I think he would have been happy to endorse it had he been here.

- To aim at *character* rather than comfort
- To foster *community* rather than commuting
- To stand for *confrontation* on issues of truth rather than compromise

The Francis Schaeffer Institute in St. Louis is clearly motivated by it. My own fledgling work in Christian Heritage in Cambridge also tries to reflect it—and doubtless dozens of other organizations like it which are unknown and unsung.

But, if the truth be told, this same vision guides and inspires countless individuals in many countries who never saw or heard Schaeffer in person. They respect him for his stand on truth; they resonate with him in his simple authenticity; they long that God would use them in their own moment of history as he used Schaeffer in his—may their number increase.

29. David Wells, *God in the Wasteland* (Grand Rapids: Eerdmans, 1994), 223.

4

Francis Schaeffer: His Legacy and His Influence on Evangelicalism

JERRAM BARRS

PERHAPS THE BEST way I can begin to speak about the legacy of Francis Schaeffer is to tell a brief story about the founding of the Francis Schaeffer Institute at Covenant Theological Seminary in St. Louis, where I have been a professor for the past twenty years. I tell this story because I know it best, but I know that this story could be multiplied many times around the world, and each story would give another facet of the legacy of Francis and Edith Schaeffer.

First I need to give a little personal history. I first met Francis Schaeffer at the time while I was an undergraduate at Manchester University in the north of England and while I was still an unbeliever. Earlier I spoke briefly about how God used Michael Tymchak to bring me to faith. Michael had studied at L'Abri in Switzerland, and there he had been greatly impacted by Schaeffer's approach to apologetics and by his life and ministry. Michael's life over 40 years later continues to be a powerful story of Schaeffer's legacy. Back in the late 60s when I met Michael he sometimes led Bible studies, sometimes had discussions, and sometimes used to play tapes of recorded lectures by Francis Schaeffer in his apartment and invite friends, both believers and unbelievers, to those evening meetings. He also invited Schaeffer to come and give a lecture at Manchester University—a lecture I attended as a non-Christian who was just beginning to wake up to the amazing answers the Christian faith gives to the questions of life. I will never forget that evening.

I had gone to university full of questions about life, eager to study and to learn, and optimistic that I would find answers to my questions at this famous center of human learning and wisdom. I was studying English literature because I love poetry, fiction, and drama, and because all great literature addresses the deepest questions and struggles of human life. It was this love for literature and my sense that studying literature would give me the key to open up the meaning of life that had sent me to Manchester with such enthusiasm and such confidence.

How naïve I was! Within a few weeks of arriving at the university and beginning to attend classes I discovered that my professors were completely uninterested in my questions. Most of them treated great literature as a series of exercises in the study of form, of historical influence, and of social impact, but seemed completely unconcerned about the meaning of texts and the author's interactions with the most basic challenges of human life in this world. Something beautiful and full of life was being turned to ashes in my classes, and this arid approach to the great works of literature led first to deep disenchantment, and then very quickly to a sense of despair and absurdity and a readiness to kill myself.

This brings me back to Schaeffer's lecture. He gave one of his overviews of Western thought and culture—a two-hour sketch of the history of ideas about God, about human life, about meaning and moral order. Schaeffer took the ideas of literature and the arts with the utmost seriousness. I was riveted and enchanted. What he said was like a beacon of light illuminating a landscape—a landscape my professors seemed determined to ignore. The things I was reading and studying began to make sense. Of course Schaeffer was not a technical expert in the areas about which he spoke—he never claimed to be. However, his approach was far more respectful of the intentions of the artists and writers of whom he spoke than was the approach of my professors. He was far more interested in what artists and writers were trying to communicate through their work than were my professors. And, in addition, he pointed to answers to the questions that all great literature and art raises about our human life here in this world. Those answers, he claimed, were to be found in God's revelation of himself to us in creation, in his Word, and through his Son.

It was a few months after hearing this lecture that I became a believer in Christ, in November 1966; then just a few months after that I graduated from Manchester, in June 1967. I had no idea what to do with my life, for God had turned my life completely around—I had become a new creature and the whole world was a new creation and had become full of meaning to me. Michael suggested that I go over to L'Abri in Switzerland, so the day after graduation I left my parents' home in the south of England and started hitchhiking my way to the Schaeffers' home in the Swiss Alps. I had no money to go by train or bus or plane or any other form of paid transport.

The Thursday morning I left home I prayed that if God wanted me to go to L'Abri I would get good rides. After about an hour I was stuck on a very minor road about thirty miles from my home, a road with very little traffic and away from all the major coastal routes. Then someone stopped to offer me a ride. It turned out that he was a Christian, a student at Cambridge University. It also turned out that he had just heard Schaeffer giving a lecture there a couple of weeks earlier, so he knew about L'Abri. It also turned out that he had taken a brief detour off the main road but was in fact heading for one of the ports to take a ferry across the English Channel on his way to Vienna, Austria. I was with him for two full days—that first day across England and to the port of Dover and then the ferry to Ostend in Belgium, a night at a youth hostel in Belgium, and then a long drive the next day down along the Rhine through Germany to Basel in Switzerland. There I spent the next night, and my driver went on his way to Vienna. The next morning it was just a few hours by courtesy of three quick hitched rides from Basel up to Huemoz and L'Abri in time for Saturday lunch. I was a very young believer and I had a strong sense that God clearly had something in mind for me in getting me there so easily.

I arrived there around June 12, 1967. My initial two-week stay turned into a year and into me becoming Edith Schaeffer's cook and gardener. I met Vicki there that September and we were engaged in October and married in December. She was from California and was working there as Schaeffer's secretary—doing his correspondence and typing up the manuscripts of *The God Who Is There* and *Escape From Reason*. Schaeffer encouraged me to attend Covenant Seminary, so we moved to St. Louis in the summer of 1968 and I graduated in 1971. We then went to join Ranald and Susan Macaulay at the English L'Abri, which had begun earlier that year. We served there till December 1988 when we came to Covenant in St. Louis to teach at the seminary. Our lives, like the lives of countless thousands of other people, had been profoundly impacted by the work of Francis and Edith Schaeffer.

When I arrived at Covenant Seminary, I had come because I felt constrained to be involved in teaching apologetics to pastors and those training for ministry. I had observed that the evangelical movement was, as much of it still is, in a general retreat into its own subculture. There is such a widespread fear of the growing forces of secularism and postmodernism that the response of many Christians has been to withdraw into the Christian community for protection by keeping a safe distance between unbelievers and us. The result of this retreat is that we create not a genuine counterculture, but a Christian "corner culture" with its own separate life and even its own language. Non-Christians perceive us as "religious" rather than as those committed to truth. We often make a dichotomy between the sacred and the secular, which leaves many unprepared to lead distinctively Christian lives at home or in the workplace. One of the most destructive consequences of all this is the "us versus them" mentality that many Christians have toward unbelievers. This makes evangelism very difficult, for evangelism becomes raids from behind our walls followed by rapid retreats. Because of working with Schaeffer, I had a passionate longing to take some of what I had seen in him, and heard from him, and put it into practice on a seminary campus. I had a longing to live it and to teach it to those going into ministry themselves, so that they could in turn be models and lead and teach others.

Shortly after arriving at Covenant I was asked by the administration and faculty if I would start the Francis Schaeffer Institute.

I said: "Yes, I will, if Edith Schaeffer is in agreement." Edith gladly agreed and came to stay with us and to give an address at the formal opening of the institute in early 1989.

I had to ask myself this question: "If we are going to have a Francis Schaeffer Institute, then it must be shaped by the ministry of Francis and Edith; otherwise, I am not prepared to do this. I cannot start with programs and ministry. Rather, I have to set down what are the main things that I learned from them. What are the central characteristics of their ministry? What were the ideas and way of life that were at the heart of all they taught and sought to live?" To express this matter another way, I was asking the question: "What is at the heart of their legacy?" I came up with a basic statement and then shared this with my former colleagues in L'Abri, who liked it and helped me develop it. It was adopted by the seminary and by L'Abri Fellowship itself, as expressing the heart of the Schaeffers' ministry, their legacy to us all. Here it is, set out in eight simple points.

1. Devotion to Christ and a Reality of Prayer as We Live in Daily Dependence upon the Lord

Francis Schaeffer would often say that the heart of Christianity is the relationship between the Bridegroom and the Bride: the love that Christ has shown us in giving himself up to death on the cross as the substitute for our sins, and the love we ought to show to him as our hearts are overwhelmed by gratitude for all he has done and continues to do for us. Without the centrality of this love, Christianity can and will degenerate into a form of godliness without its power. Francis Schaeffer believed that one of the most important things he wrote was the essay, "The Secret of Power and the Enjoyment of the Lord," published in the early 1950s.

This was written as a response to the lack of spiritual power, the lack of devotional literature and new hymns, the ugliness in personal relationships, and the striving for status and leadership that increasingly characterized the separated movement of which he was a part. He came out of this dark period of his life with a renewed conviction of the truth of the gospel and also with a new emphasis on the finished work of Christ as the basis, not only for justification, but also for sanctification.

We are called to live with the love of Christ as the motivating force of our inner being, and actively to depend on the power of God as we seek to serve and obey him. Prayer, moment by moment prayer, is to characterize the people of God, for we are living in a supernatural universe, one open at all times to God's intervention in our lives and in this world. It was this conviction that led Francis and Edith to believe that L'Abri should be a demonstration of God's existence and of the truth of Christianity as those in the work depend on him day by day and as he graciously answered their prayers.

2. Confidence in Biblical Truth

The Scriptures of the Old and New Testaments describe themselves as revelation, communication in language, from the infinite personal God to us his creatures. The Bible claims divine inspiration for all that it affirms, and therefore also claims to be infallible and inerrant in its teaching. This is true whether it is addressing matters of faith and practice or matters of history and the cosmos.

The Bible was, of course, written by human authors and should be read, as with any other book, according to the rules of historical-grammatical exegesis. Yet, this book is the living

Word of God, able to make us wise to salvation and sufficient to teach us all we need to know for life and godliness.

3. The Reality of the Fall

The disobedience of Adam and Eve, their rebellion against God at the earliest stage of human history, brought the whole race as their descendants into a state of sin and judgment. The reality of this fall expresses itself in seven separations:

1. God in his perfect righteousness can have nothing to do with evil and is, therefore, justly angry with us his creatures. This wrath of God is daily experienced by us and our fellows, for we were created for loving fellowship with our Maker, and yet we sense his just indignation against us, an indignation which will last eternally for those not reconciled to him through Christ.
2. We are those whose hearts are filled with pride and self-worship rather than humble devotion to the Lord. There is deep reluctance within us to love and serve our Creator, for we are alienated from him.
3. We are also alienated from ourselves; that is, within each one of us we find the disintegrating power of sin. We do not faithfully express God's holiness and so we experience guilt and shame. We are not what we should be, we are unable to do what we wish, nor do we even accurately know what is deep in our own hearts. This inner brokenness demonstrates itself in the extremes of inordinate self-love and self-hatred and in psychological disorder.
4. This separation within our own persons is also expressed in our bodies. Pain, sickness, and the debility that comes with advancing age demonstrate this physical corruption.

Death, our final enemy, manifests this reality most fully as it tears apart body and spirit and brings our bodies down to the grave.

5. We are alienated from each other. Even in our most cherished relationships—marriage, family, and friendship—we discover ugly passions in our hearts: pride, jealousy, envy, resentment, bitterness, and hatred. These passions are at work in every facet of human society—in hostility between individuals, social groups, classes, races, and nations. This inner enmity may break out in discrimination, violence, warfare, and even genocide.

6. There is separation between us and creation around us. Instead of our dominion being made known in faithful stewardship of the earth, we pollute and damage our environment and recklessly destroy our fellow creatures.

7. Even creation itself suffers separation as it has been subjected to the curse. The earth resists our attempts at dominion so that our daily work can be burdensome and even unproductive, and the natural order experiences disintegration and violence.

Christ, through his triumph on the cross and in his resurrection, has overcome, is overcoming, and will overcome fully all of these separations.

4. Commitment to Genuine Humanness Expressed in Servanthood and Love, and Displayed in Supernaturally Restored Relationships

Within the Trinity there have been love and personal communication through all eternity. We humans have been created in the likeness of this personal God, although our humanness has in every aspect of our nature been desperately flawed by sin and its effects. Christ, God's son, came into this world, lived as a perfect man, died, and rose again in order to restore us to fellowship with God and to overcome all the consequences of the fall in our lives.

Christ is at work restoring us to true humanness as we become conformed to his likeness by the power of the Spirit. This will mean that wherever there is true faith in Christ, there will be a life that begins to imitate the love of Christ. The apostle Paul calls us to have the mind of Christ as we think more highly of one another than of ourselves and as we give ourselves to a life of service, loving one another as Christ has loved us.

Christ is the peace between us and God and between us and one another; therefore, the divisions that so often exist between people, whether personal, cultural, racial, or economic, ought to be overcome by those who have come to know Christ. Though it will not in this age be perfect, yet in our homes and families, in our friendships and our churches, in our workplaces and neighborhoods, this supernatural restoration of relationships ought to be realized wherever there is true Christianity.

5. Commitment to Apply God's Truth to the Whole of Life and to Encourage Christians to Make a Contribution to the Wider Culture

Scripture makes no distinction between the sacred and the secular, nor does it encourage us to think that some activities, such as prayer or evangelism, are more spiritual than other activities, such as caring for children or manual labor. Rather, we are taught that Christ is the Lord of all of life and that our calling is to honor him in all that we do. We are to take captive every thought to make it obedient to Christ and to seek to serve him in every human activity.

Often Christians retreat from the wider culture believing it to be completely dominated by ideas and practices that are contrary to God's commandments. Christians feel that developing our own corner culture will provide protection from the world for us and our children but, by this, society is abandoned to go its wicked way. Yet, God has not abandoned the human race. Humans all still bear the divine image, and therefore his glory can still be perceived in all human cultures despite the terrible corruptions of sin. Christians are called by the Lord not to withdraw from the world but to be in it, living as salt and light in it, rejoicing in all that is good in human society, and committing ourselves to make a difference in our own small way in whatever calling we are placed by the Lord.

6. The Appreciation of God's Gifts in All of Life

God is the maker and giver of every good gift. The universe is filled with the display of his imagination and his delight in creating what is good, beautiful, and true. We are called to enjoy God's creation, and as those made in his image, we are to delight in using body, mind, and imagination to express our own creativity and to enrich the lives of others as we do. Whether it is the appreciation of great art in all the varied disciplines, or whether it is the "hidden art" of serving a well-prepared meal, or digging a ditch, we should honor, and be thankful for the depth and richness that art brings to our lives.

7. The Need to Understand the Culture We Live in and Communicate to It

Christ became incarnate in a particular culture at a particular time in history. He knew his contemporaries because he was one with them, raised and educated as they were, shaped by the same ideas and customs, and yet he lived in obedience to his Father's will in all that he thought and said and did. On every page of the Gospels we see his deep knowledge and understanding of the times in which he lived and of the people to whom he sought to make known the good news of the kingdom.

To resist the ideas and practices of the culture in which we live, we have to understand them and bring them before the bar of Scripture. Reflections on the Word and on the world are necessary, both for holy living and also for wise communication of the gospel to those around us. Paul spoke the same truth but he presented it in different ways depending on whether he was in a synagogue with Jews and God-fearing Gentiles, or on Mars Hill with pagans. To communicate faithfully we have to work at understanding the intellectual climate of the times in which we live, and we need to give ourselves to people in love if we want to know what idols captivate the hearts of our contemporaries.

8. The Preparedness to Give Honest Answers to Honest Questions in Such a Way That the Unbeliever May Be Faced with the Truth Claims of Christianity

Because Christianity is the truth, people should be encouraged to ask the questions that trouble them. Paul reminds us that the weapons we fight with are not the weapons of this world, and that therefore they have divine power to demolish strongholds. God has made truth known in his Word, and so we may urge the unbeliever and the believer to come to Scripture with their questions. There will always be good and sufficient answers available for those who seek with an open heart and mind. This is so, whether we desire to show that a biblical worldview makes sense of life in a way that no other worldview does, or whether we wish to defend the historical truth of the biblical revelation.

All people are rebels against God in their hearts and minds, so we recognize that the task of evangelism is not simply a matter of persuading people of the truth of the Christian message. We present the truth and the reasons for believing it, and at the same time we pray for the Holy Spirit to humble the mind and heart of the hearer in order that he or she might be open to the truth and be convinced by it.

These eight points set out what I believe to be the fundamental elements of the Schaeffers' legacy to us all. They are not of course original to them, for these points are simply an elaboration of some of the most basic elements of faithful biblical Christianity. But that is why these points are so significant and that is why the Schaeffers' legacy is one that we can cherish.

I want to add a final footnote to this personal story of my own indebtedness to the work that God did in the lives of Francis and Edith Schaeffer. Everywhere I travel in the world I meet people and have the privilege of seeing ministries that owe this same kind of debt to the faithful teaching and lives of the Schaeffers. This past year I have been teaching in Japan, in Brazil, in Hungary to people from many European countries, as well as in England and in many places here in the United States. Every time I go anywhere, I meet people who were converted through the Schaeffers' ministry or whose lives and service for the Lord have been profoundly impacted by their ministry. In Japan six weeks ago I taught a seminary class where one of the pastors and several other students were members of a church called the L'Abri Bible Church. The young pastor was so deeply impacted by the teaching of Schaeffer that he wanted to honor his legacy by giving the church he pastors that particular name. It is this profound indebtedness to the Schaeffers' grasp of foundational biblical truth that is their most significant legacy.

5

Sentimentality:
Significance
for Apologetics

DICK KEYES

THIS CHAPTER will not be about Francis Schaeffer directly. Instead, I will give one example of the many sorts of things that reflect the thinking of Schaeffer as applied today. I will focus on how we think as we try with God's help to continue his vision for a broad-reaching cultural apologetic and for clarifying the healing power of the gospel for people today. I will look at sentimentality as a serious, but largely unnoticed threat to the Christian faith. It may seem strange to you to raise sentimentality as anything but a frivolous pop-culture phenomenon, but as we progress, I think you will see its significance. Having spent

Editor's note: Rather than being about Schaeffer in particular, this chapter presents an analysis of a present influential idea in culture in typical Schaeffer fashion. It is a practical demonstration of how one might engage the ideas of culture today from a Christian worldview.

a lot of time thinking and writing about cynicism,[1] I found I was always bumping into the sentimentalist in the gun sights of the cynic, the cynic's sworn enemy and yet favorite, perhaps needed, target. In certain ways they are opposite poles. Oscar Wilde once quipped that sentimentality is what happens when cynicism goes on a bank holiday.

Sentimentality presents two kinds of problems for Christians. First, if sentimentality has seduced the Christian community, that itself is a serious enough problem to Christian integrity. But insofar as this seduction has happened, it then becomes a reliable turnoff to honest people who are investigating whether truth might be found in Jesus Christ. They will conclude that faith in Christ is only sentimentality, and scorn it. It has become a negative apologetic in the sense that it contributes to the implausibility of Christ in the public mind. Second, it presents a challenge to Christian apologetics in that the sentimental person who is not a Christian will have built-in filters and barriers to real Christian belief which will block him or her from taking Christ seriously.

Let me first describe what I mean by the word "sentimentality," and then develop it more fully. I am indebted to Jeremy S. Begbie[2] for this formulation of the elements of sentimentality and for his excellent bibliography.

First, sentimentality sees a world without sin, evil, brokenness, ugliness, cruelty, complexity, or confusion. These unpleasant things are denied, trivialized, or euphemized. It is a world of niceness, warmth, harmony, and simplicity. Second, sentimentality is self-referential emotion. It is a turning of the feelings back on them-

---

1. Dick Keyes, *Seeing Through Cynicism: A Reconsideration of the Power of Suspicion* (Downers Grove, IL: InterVarsity, 2006).

2. Jeremy S. Begbie, "Beauty, Sentimentality and the Arts," in *The Beauty of God*, ed. Daniel J. Treier, Mark Husbands, and Roger Lundin (Downers Grove, IL: InterVarsity, 2007).

selves, feeling about your feeling. This means that people in the grip of sentimentality who think they are in love may actually not so much love another person, as love their own emotions about that other person. Their love may be largely for what the other person does to and for them. Third, sentimental emotions do not result in responsible action. This makes sense if feelings are self-referential (about me, not the outside world). Sentimental emotions distract and anesthetize us from what might be appropriate responses, especially if those responses are costly or inconvenient.

When all these three aspects of sentimentality are together, they form a kind of twisted coherence, each of the three feeding the others. Sentimentality is not just found in stores that sell Hallmark cards, or in 1940s movies. This full form of sentimentality is a very powerful force throughout our society.

THE CHARACTER OF SENTIMENTALITY

Sentimentality is threatened by seeing evil clearly in its danger, ugliness, cruelty, guilt, shame, and emptiness. The sentimentalist is averse to the idea that all people have a natural capacity for evil. The ability to see the world through a lens of innocence and niceness and denial of sin is not hard to do when you can simply choose what you want to look at and what you do not want to look at, listen to, and not listen to. The modern world of entertainment and the Internet enables us to control what we want to see and hear to a new degree, and so is able to nurture the self-deception of our choice.

Denial or Evasion of Evil and Brokenness

A classic example of the political use of sentimentality is the Nazi propaganda machine in the 1930s devised by Goebbels. He had a very self-conscious approach to music on the radio, playing morning, afternoon, and evening. It was for the most part not the Wagner or militaristic marches that one might expect. It was overwhelmingly sweet, syrupy love songs, hour after hour, year after year, as Hitler was turning the country into a police state built on a racist nightmare. What better distraction, especially as it is perceived as normal?

If you read Huxley's *Brave New World*, his future dystopia, you see that people are not controlled by force, fear, or threat. They were controlled by pleasure, endless sentimental clichés, happy upbeat slogans, and elaborate positive conditioning, with a powerful feel-good drug as a backup.

Media sentimentality is vast and it starts early. Children are told by Barney that the world is wonderful, that everybody loves them, and that they can have what they want by wishing for it. Is that what we want our children to believe? Walt Disney has given us, in the words of one scholar, a world "without dirt, cruelty, or complexity." It is also without God or church, but with plenty of niceness, simplicity, optimism, and superb marketing.

If you have watched public TV fund-raising programs, you may have seen a concert by James Taylor to celebrate his long career. I do not want to evaluate him as a singer-songwriter here, but what struck me was that the whole concert built toward the end when it was promised that he would sing "Fire and Rain," the song that made his reputation number three on the charts in 1970, but which you can still hear regularly in your dentist office, in an airport, or in an elevator (thirty-nine years later!). It is a song about the suicide of a good friend, heroin addiction and withdrawal, clinical depression for which he was hospitalized several times, and the collapse of his dreams of a career. When he finally came to sing it at this concert in 2006, he sang it with a grin on his face from ear to ear, insofar as anyone can sing and smile at the same time. He was singing it to an audience that was also beaming and swaying with the music. It was a nostalgia bath, completely disconnected from the lyrics and life experience of the song. I thought, "This is a high point of musical sentimentality," even for one who has become the king of airport music. Sentimentality filters out what is upsetting and evil in the world and stimulates emotions that are comforting, soothing, and positive.

How many people intentionally maintain a total diet of stories in film and print that have impossibly unrealistic happy endings? This amounts to not facing or dealing with the brokenness that is in me, in my neighbor, or in the world. It is a self-induced self-deception.

Self-Referential Emotion

The philosopher Roger Scruton wrote: "Sentimentality is that peculiarly human vice which consists in directing your emotions toward your own emotions, so as to be the subject of a story told by yourself."[3] What looks like feelings for another, really have me as their object.

Think about Tennyson's famous poem, "In Memoriam." It is one of the great poems of the nineteenth century. It is a long poem, forty to fifty pages. It is about the death of Tennyson's closest friend, Arthur Hallam, at twenty-two years of age. Hallam had been Tennyson's counselor and his sister's fiancé. It shook Tennyson and his faith to the core. But in this long poem, you learn nothing about Arthur Hallam himself. It is all about Tennyson. It is about Tennyson's grief, Tennyson's suffering, and the trials of Tennyson's faith. It is almost entirely self-referential.

3. Roger Scruton, *Gentle Regrets* (New York: Continuum Books, 2005), 102.

Consider Princess Diana's funeral. There were millions of people deeply moved at her death, bringing mountains of flowers. In the thousands of interviews, people spoke not so much about Princess Diana herself, but about their own feelings about her death. It was as if her death was something that had happened to *them*. They wanted to talk about how it made them feel. If you have seen the Helen Mirren film, "The Queen," you see the polarization between the stoical royal family on the one side, and the people on the other, whose media-driven sentimentalism mystified the queen and her husband. The royal family had not understood "conspicuous compassion," the pleasure of a public demonstration or display of sorrow, compassion, or any strong emotion. The buzz of crying on TV makes people feel good about themselves, and also connected to others who are crying on TV for the same reason.

We live in a society where everything is scripted. In the world of politicians and celebrities, every word, every move is focus-group tested and spun. Think of how excited journalists get when they catch a politician saying something when he did not know the microphone was still turned on! In this world of spin and contrivance, we like to think that the one part of life that is protected from prior scripting is our own emotions, which are spontaneous, free, authentic, uniquely our own.

But what we hear from the critics of sentimentality is, "Not so fast. Don't you see that our sentimentalized society teaches you what to feel?" It teaches you what you need to feel in order to feel good about yourself. If you feel this way, then it is OK to respect yourself.[4] Stjepan Mestrovic argues in *Postemotional Society* that our real and authentic emotions are there, but are buried under the feelings that we feel we are

4. Stjepan G. Mestrovic, *Postemotional Society* (Thousand Oaks, CA: Sage Publications, 1997), 43–68.

meant to feel in whatever situation we are in. So, even though so much emphasis is put on emotion, we are in a postemotional society.[5] Scruton references T. S. Eliot's critical essays as pointing out that "sentimentality causes us not merely to write in clichés, but to *feel* in clichés too, lest we be troubled by the truth of our condition."[6] D. H. Lawrence wrote one of the classic descriptions of sentimentalism:

> Sentimentalism is the working off on yourself of feelings you haven't really got. We all *want* to have certain feelings: feelings of love, of passionate sex, of kindliness, and so forth. Very few people really feel love, or sex passion, or kindliness, or anything else that goes all that deep. So the masses just fake these feelings inside themselves. Faked feelings! The world is all gummy with them. They are better than real feeling, because you can spit them out when you brush your teeth; and then tomorrow you can fake them afresh.[7]

One of the standard "put-downs" for sentimentalism in the arts is "kitsch." Lines are hard to draw here between individual taste and value that transcends taste, so it is easy to step on toes. Let me start with the most basic. Most lawn ornaments are kitsch. The classic kitsch icon is the plastic pink flamingo. Velvet Elvis portraits are kitsch, as are velvet portraits of John Wayne, Dale Earnhardt, and Jesus. Some would consider the paintings of Thomas Kinkade to be kitsch—but that usually produces an argument.

5. Ibid., 73–78.
6. Roger Scruton, *An Intelligent Person's Guide to Modern Culture* (South Bend, IN: St. Augustine's Press, 2000), 80.
7. D. H. Lawrence, *Selected Essays* (London: Penguin, 1954), 224; quoted in Ian Robinson, "Faking Emotion, Sentimentality in Modern Literature," in *Faking It*, ed. Digby Anderson and Peter Mullen (London: Penguin Books, 1998), 121.

The word "kitsch" seems to come from a verb in a German dialect which originally meant the manure and mud scraped up from the street. Then it started to be used in the late nineteenth century to describe cheesy, slapped-together attempts at art sold cheap. It was for those who knew no better but who got a false sense of their own sophistication from thinking that they now owned "art." It started to come into use in English in a big way in the 1930s.

Kitsch is usually mass produced, poor quality, and a shallow substitute for real art, driven by the needs of the market. It is commercial, clichéd, trite, designed to provide an emotional uplift and the illusion of a social connection of warmth and niceness with others. The content of kitsch is sentimental. It tries to help you fake a desired emotion that it has not really earned. It does not deal with serious thought or reflection, either by its creator or by the viewer. It does not challenge or stretch us. It tries to give us a cheap comfort and ease, warm feelings of niceness. It is what people produce when they aim at beauty without concern for truth and have no room for complexity, contradiction, or evil. Of course the place of kitsch in advertising is enormous.

Emotion Without Appropriate, Costly Response

There is a famous story from the Victorian era, attributed to various people, of a gentleman and his wife who go to the theater in the city in their carriage on a very cold and snowy night. They are profoundly moved by the play and are both in tears from the story of injustice and suffering callously inflicted on poor people who were helpless to resist it. When the play is over, they come out of the theater and they discover that their coachman, because he was almost frozen to death waiting for them, had neglected to sweep the snow off the step of the carriage. The gentleman screams at him and proceeds to whip him with the horsewhip. This is the third element of sentimentality, the problem of disconnection between sentimental feelings and appropriate real-life behavior.

The problem is not with the presence of emotion, even very strong emotion. It is what happens to that emotion. How is it expressed? It had become somehow self-indulgent in its self-reference, disconnected from the rest of the world. Clichés can be expressions of feeling, maybe strong feeling, but with no intention for action: "I'll always be there for you," "You mean more to me than you'll ever know" *can* be perfectly sincere, but can also be sentimental clichés, false promises leading to nothing. Oscar Wilde wrote that the sentimentalist "desires to have the luxury of an emotion without paying for it . . . they always try to get their emotion on credit, and refuse to pay the bill when it comes in."[8]

Think about the vast popularity of TV news. What is it designed to do? Of course it is designed to entertain in order to make money, which it can only do by keeping you from changing channels. But how does it keep you from changing channels? Much of the TV news is designed to make you feel good about yourself for feeling bad.[9] TV news is designed to engage your emotions, not that you would do anything about the news (how could you possibly?), but that you would feel right and good about feeling those things—grief, outrage, compassion,

8. Oscar Wilde, "Letter to Lord Alfred Douglas," in *The Letters of Oscar Wilde*, ed. Rupert Hart-Davis (London: Harcourt, Brace & World, 1962), 501; quoted in Jeremy S. Begbie, "Beauty, Sentimentality and the Arts," in *The Beauty of God*, ed. Daniel J. Treier, Mark Husbands, and Roger Lundin (Downers Grove,IL: InterVarsity, 2007), 52.

9. Mark Steyn, "All Venusians Now, Sentimentality in Media," in *Faking It*, ed. Digby Anderson and Peter Mullen (London: Penguin Books, 1998), 165–67.

and empathy. Could it be that some TV news builds feelings of satisfaction about myself for feeling compassion about the victims of murder, assassination, flood, earthquake . . . much more than it encourages actual concern or action for the people who are hurt?

We can see this aspect of sentimentality identified, exposed, and skewered in many places in the Bible. It is no good to speak and feel lovely platitudes and clichés about love, service, compassion, sensitivity, suffering, pity, justice, and beauty, but do nothing to pursue these goals or virtues or mitigate the suffering of others. Think of 1 John 3:18, "Let us love, not in word or speech, but in truth and action." It is quite possible to love just in words, not in actions.

One of the most thorough repudiations of sentimentality comes from the Letter of James, 2:15–16: "If a brother or sister is naked and lacks daily food, and one of you says to them, 'Go in peace; keep warm and eat your fill,' and yet you do not supply their bodily needs, what is the good of that?" James says to the person who does this that his or her faith is dead. You see, it is very possible to have wonderful sentiments for others in their suffering—of peace, warmth, and good nourishment—but *do* nothing to help them. James nails sentimentality here on all its three counts: (1) It is not taking the evil of another's suffering seriously as evil; (2) It is being pleased with your own emotional response of compassion; (3) It is allowing a person to go away distraught, cold, and hungry while you have done nothing except to feel compassionate feelings. This is dead faith.

Christianity and Sentimentality in Collision

If we evaluate the defining characteristics of sentimentality—denial or trivializing of evil, self-referential emotional life, and emotion not leading to responses of action—it is a profound denial or betrayal of the Christian faith. Yet we may not notice the depth of this denial because sentimentality is all about niceness.

I will note two particular problems that this poses for the Christian faith. First, if sentimentality has corrupted the Christian community, people of integrity who are searching for truth are likely to conclude that the Christian faith is sentimental at its core, and they will turn away in disillusionment or scorn. They will say, "These people have no honesty. They are playing their own comfortable little game with the church as their private club and God as their crutch." Sentimentality among Christians encourages the reaction of cynicism as well. Second, for the person who is sentimental and not a Christian, his sentimentality itself will block him from seeing the need to take Christ seriously.

WHEN CHRISTIANITY IS SEDUCED BY SENTIMENTALISM

You might think that since the collision between the basic ideas of Christianity and those of sentimentalism is so violent, that the Christian community would be an oasis in the world, free from sentimentalism. Well, it is not. This costs Christians deeply. I will illustrate this by reviewing the three aspects of sentimentality as it appears within Christian experience.

See No Evil

There was an interesting editorial by ethicist David Gushee, titled, "How to Create Cynics." Remember that cynicism is the opposite extreme from sentimentality. I will quote it at some length.

> One of the greatest causes of cynicism among Christians is the way we lather God-talk over our lives in order to obscure realities we consider too painful to discuss directly.
>
> Consider this example from church life (though such situations are not confined to local churches). A minister is not happy in his place of service. He wonders whether he was right in accepting this call in the first place. He has dealt with painful personality conflicts, constant power struggles, and criticism. Now he is leaving. He is leaving because he can't take it anymore. His future is most uncertain.
>
> But he believes that he can't say any of these things. There is an unwritten Code in the church (and not just this church) that dictates how a minister says goodbye. So he says, "God spoke to me and is leading me to a different place of service at this time. I appreciate the opportunity to be your pastor. I now must move on to wherever God leads me next."
>
> Everybody on the inside of the situation knows what these words really mean: "I am miserable here. I can't take it anymore. At this point, I would rather be unemployed than continue to serve here. I'm not sure exactly where God is in all of this, but in any case, I know that I must move on. I sure wish you would deal with the issues that have led me to this point, but I won't tell you what those are, so I doubt that you will actually deal with them."[10]

What he is saying—without actually using the word "sentimentalism"—is that many Christians can't stand to face doubt,

---

10. David Gushee, "How to Create Cynics," *Christianity Today*, September (2006): 114.

uncertainty, or conflict in areas close to their faith, so they have a sentimental language code that filters them out and replaces them with warm, nice euphemisms. It is not the doubts, uncertainties, and conflicts that create cynics as much as it is the denials and euphemisms of the code.

Here is the apologetic problem. People suspect Christians are being dishonest. The problem is that they are right. And what is it that we show the world if Christian people can't be honest about living as Christian people? We are the ones who are meant to believe in sin. How should we expect non-Christian people to believe in sin if we live as if we can only euphemize and deny it in ourselves? It looks like there is something wrong with the Christian faith itself, so it becomes less credible in the mind of the searching person.

Self-Reference

There is very dangerous ground for sliding into cynicism from a different direction. I am thinking of D. H. Lawrence's claim that we tend to fake the feelings that we wish were real. We don't have them as real feelings but we want them, so we fake them. The world is all gummy with them.

Do you think that sometimes, every once in a great while, we witness faked feelings of worship or love for God? Do you think you have ever seen faked feelings of intimacy with God? Do we even do it sometimes ourselves? This is a danger in evangelical faith because a great emphasis is put on the intimacy of my individual walk with God (to the sacrifice of the breadth of the faith). Christian literature and contemporary music are filled with such glowing descriptions of life-changing encounters with the Lord, almost as if they happen once a month. I feel the need to caution, "Let's make sure that we keep it real. Nobody's fooling God. And if it isn't real, it's not helping anyone."

Christian Nonengagement in the Society That We Say We Care About

There is no time here to talk of the Christian noninvolvement in issues of public concern. Too often the Christian community has privatized and withdrawn from wider society into its own sacred tribal subculture. However, there has been great progress in the other direction in the last thirty years, and an encouraging desire among many evangelical Christians to engage in their wider society as followers of Christ. But sentimentality still resists this spirit of Christian involvement in the world and, if we do not reject sentimentality, it will keep us on the sidelines. By contrast, if we face up to and deal with sin and evil honestly, even when it is uncomfortable, complicated, and hard work, that is a very powerful testimony to God's truth.

ENGAGEMENT WITH SENTIMENTAL PEOPLE

We need to be clear here about the "see no evil" idea. It sidesteps the whole biblical diagnosis of the human problem of evil when it is found within us, where it is called sin. When sin is denied, trivialized, or euphemized, the basic fabric of the Christian theology of redemption or salvation becomes superfluous and unnecessary. Sin is the problem to which the coming of Jesus and his death and resurrection were the solution. If sin is not an issue, then the cross in its atoning work becomes an embarrassment. But, it is so negative, so crude, so barbaric, and punitive. Who needs it? It is irrelevant, an optional salvation which no one really needs. I always remember a conversation with one of our students who said, "I didn't ask Jesus to die for me, I think that's highly manipulative!" I had to say that he would be entirely right—if sin was not a serious problem.

Where Are Sentimental People in the Light of the Gospel?

As Christians, we need to be clear about self-referential emotions also. If they are the center of our lives, we miss the importance of the whole God-created world out there—a world that God takes very seriously. He made it. We often find people who have "no sense of other." Whatever happens in their lives is only grasped in terms of how it impacts them and makes them feel. A friend totals his car and I respond, "Oh, what a bummer, I was going to borrow his car next weekend!"

The Christian faith, by comparison, says there is a real world out there, outside your head, which, along with the vast creation, includes a lot of people who are precious to God because they are made in his image just as we are. There is a real, solid world out there which will push back if we ignore its givenness and the evil found in it.

Sentimentality's Filters

Sentimentality can filter out any sense of dissonance—anxiety, fear, guilt, shame, alienation, loneliness, and meaninglessness that might be coming from God. So the sentimental person is protected from experiencing any urgency or seriousness about these dissonant feelings. There is no need to change, rethink, much less to repent. Sentimentality can domesticate all these feelings which can be coming from a collision with reality itself or from God's pressure put on someone trying to live without God. Sentimentality can homogenize them all by distraction and displacement into feelings of warmth, comfort, niceness, and superficiality.

When Jesus came back to his hometown of Nazareth, the people asked him to preach at the synagogue on the Sabbath (Luke 4:16–30). He read from Isaiah about the coming of the Messiah, and then said to the people that the very prophecy had been fulfilled in their hearing. What he was saying was: "Your long-awaited Messiah is now here, right in front of your eyes, in your presence. I am the one. The time is now."

You might have thought they would have responded: "Really? What do we do? Where do we go? Praise God, at last he has heard our prayers!" On the other hand they might have said, "You're not him. You must be a fake. We know who you are. We knew you when you were just a kid." His words called for radical commitment and action—one way or the other.

But what did they say? "He has such a nice way with words. He is so well-spoken." They filtered out anything that would have demanded something hard of them, even serious thinking about the teaching of the Bible. Jesus then pushed them until he pushed through their sentimentality—but then they chased him out of town and tried to throw him off a cliff.

A Place of Contact

Sentimentalists are likely to be out of reach of Christian proclamation and argument, just as the residents of Nazareth were. They are distracted from the issues that would make them look seriously to the biblical God on his own terms. But reality that is denied still pushes back. We must be aware of trying to encourage that "push-back" and help them understand it. The reality of the world itself and its brokenness confronts us all, whether we like it or not.

We all know people who start worrying about God or looking for God only when things go wrong and they are disillusioned by the crash of their dreams or their idols. They may have been treated with cruelty or dishonesty, or lied to or cheated, by people they trusted. At a men's retreat at our church, we discussed what had started us searching for God with real seriousness. Again and again it turned out that death and divorce were the triggers that started us.

God's reality and the reality of his creation bring reality checks to us if we have ears to hear and eyes to see. There is a vast range of ways that the world's brokenness and our own brokenness can show cracks in our sentimental security. The prodigal son's state of bankruptcy and hunger was just such a reality check. I think an important part of apologetics in the future will be helping people understand the evil and sin that they have experienced but do not have the categories to understand.

There is another reality check to sentimentality. It is the realization that perhaps I have become a shallow person. I heard a disturbing put-down. It was, "Deep down, he is very shallow." What a terrible thing if that is true of you or me. Deep down, we are very shallow. There is no depth to us. Go as deep as you want and you still get shallowness, superficiality, self-preoccupation, vanity, triviality, and self-indulgence.

This is exactly what sentimentality does to us if we are unwilling to engage in the unpleasant, the upsetting, and the suffering of life. If we avoid life's complexity and confusion, if we can't face pain in ourselves or others, if what we feel most deeply always references ourselves, then sure enough, we have already become—deep down—very shallow.

Jesus clarified our choices. He said, "Woe to you who are laughing now, for you will mourn and weep" (Luke 6:25). We can choose to live life "laughing now" and try to keep on laughing, to live in a bubble of happiness, flippancy, and denial. Yet, Jesus maintained that this effort was doomed and would end in mourning and weeping. His other option was the beatitude: "Blessed are those who mourn, for they will be comforted" (Matt. 5:4). We can mourn the brokenness in the world, work against it in ourselves, in others, and in the world with God's help. This is a strange and paradoxical truth. It is not an invitation to mourning as complaint, self-pity, or nostalgia. It is rather a call to mourn as God himself mourns, in sadness over seeing suffering, evil, and sin, but working to change it. Jesus' promise seems to be for blessedness or fulfillment at a deep level. As we think of several of the pressure points of sentimentality, the consequences become clear.

CONCLUSION

What sort of persons do we become if we deny and trivialize our own sin? We become self-righteous, pompous, self-satisfied, self-deceived, fearful, and eventually miserable. We will alienate ourselves from others because we are always excusing or making light of our mistakes and refusing to be honest about ourselves.

What sort of persons do we become if we deny or trivialize our own suffering, anxiety, doubt, depression, anger, sense of inferiority, and inadequacy? We become fake, hollow, phony people driven by fear of discovery. A variation of this theme that we see a lot is in those who have not been able to admit doubts about God—uncertainties about their faith, or anger with God. Doubt that is denied gains enormous power as we become more phony, pretending to be good Christians.

What sort of persons do we become if we don't relate to other people in *their* suffering? Involving ourselves in others' suffering can be costly of time and energy. It means not always knowing what to say, very long conversations, or bearing heavy loads with them—all commitments that we might not be willing to make. It is easy to see why we might want to avoid other people in their suffering. But what do we become? We become more and more selfish, more shallow, more superficial, and phony in our concerns. What if our most important relationships are with our TV sets?

What sort of persons do we become if we don't honestly confront conflicts with other people? We want to keep the world a happy place, and especially have everyone in it happy with us. We become inwardly fearful people, fearing the conflicts that we have avoided. But in doing this we set ourselves up for far worse conflicts, compounded conflicts more difficult to resolve than they would have been had we faced them earlier. Those conflicts are usually forced on us when we are finally not able to run away from them. We also may end up moving a lot—socially or geographically. As conflict looms, run away so as not to have to deal with it.

These are all areas where we can help people make a reality check. People don't want to be dishonest, shallow, hollow, phony, and insensitive, without "sense of other." I have found that the challenge to something better has real traction in the lives of people who have used sentimentality to avoid God. A loss of humanness is reality pushing back.

So, we have discussed sentimentality, a subject that does not get enough press in Christian discussion, but is all over modern America and, sadly, in Christian living as well. Its apologetic significance cuts two ways. If Christians themselves are sentimental enough, it keeps real seekers away and encourages their cynicism about Christ. But also, if people are sentimental enough they will not realize their need for Christ.

In the midst of these concerns there is the great paradox of Jesus' teaching: honesty about brokenness is not only good because it is true, but that honesty is really redemptive and will draw us into a far deeper and more fulfilling life. The Christian faith makes a terrible diagnosis but brings a magnificent hope. This magnificent hope has not been at all the topic of this chapter, but freeing ourselves from sentimentality opens the way for us to understand a hope that is solid. We can't expect to skip forward over the diagnosis to embrace the hope. "Blessed are those who mourn for they shall be comforted."